The Author

Dr Clive Fletcher is Head of the Psychology Department at Goldsmiths' College, University of London. As a consultant to numerous public and private sector organisations, he has been involved in the selection of job applicants and in the training of some hundreds of interviewers. Dr Fletcher has written widely on assessment and has carried out a series of research studies on the interview and how candidates see it. He is a Fellow of the British Psychological Society and a former Chairman of its Occupational Psychology Section.

How to Face
the Interview
– and other selection procedures

CLIVE FLETCHER

UNWIN
PAPERBACKS

LONDON SYDNEY WELLINGTON

First published as *Facing The Interview* by Unwin Paperbacks 1981
Published as *How To Face The Interview* by Unwin® Paperbacks,
an imprint of Unwin Hyman Limited, in 1986
Reprinted in 1987 and 1988

UNWIN HYMAN LIMITED
15–17 Broadwick Street
London W1V 1FP

Allen & Unwin Australia Pty Ltd
8 Napier Street, North Sydney, NSW 2060, Australia

Allen & Unwin New Zealand Pty Ltd with the Port Nicholson Press
60 Cambridge Terrace, Wellington, New Zealand

British Library Cataloguing in Publication Data

Fletcher, Clive
    How to face the interview and other selection procedures
2nd ed.
1. Job hunting   2. Employment interviewing
I. Title
650.1'4   HF5382.7
ISBN 0–04–380027–0

Set in 10 on 11 point Palatino by Bedford Typesetters Ltd
and printed in Great Britain by Cox & Wyman Ltd, Reading.

Acknowledgements

I would like to thank the following individuals for their invaluable comments and advice while I was writing this book: Dr Rowan Bayne, Viv Barker, John Churchill, Dr Vic Dulewicz, and Dr James Walker. I am also indebted to two anonymous reviewers, a Principal Careers Officer and a careers teacher, for their helpful suggestions on earlier drafts of the book.

Contents

1

A Positive Approach to the Interview

The Widespread Use of Interviews for Selection

The interview is still by far the most commonly used method for assessing a person's suitability for a job. In the USA, it has been shown that 99 per cent of companies use this technique when hiring staff, and the equivalent figure for Britain is much the same. Only in the case of some unskilled jobs do organisations seem to feel that they can afford to do without the interview. Reliance on interviews as a way of fitting square pegs into square holes does not stop there, either, as this same technique is widely used in making promotion decisions too. So most of us will have the experience of being interviewed – for places at college, for jobs, for promotions and so on – not just once, but many times. The whole direction of our lives may be altered by success or failure in an interview that can be as short as 15 minutes or as long as three hours. The outcome can be just as important to the organisation concerned; if they make a bad decision, they may be stuck with an unsuitable employee for years. In view of the importance to both sides, it is reasonable to ask whether or not the interview is a good way of selecting people for jobs.

Are They Effective?

With countless thousands of interviews being conducted each year, it is not surprising to find that there have been many research studies aimed at finding out just how good interview judgements are. There are two approaches to this:

* The first is to see whether or not different interviewers who (separately) interview the same people come to much the same assessments of them. One of the earliest studies of this kind was done in the 1920s, and involved 12 sales managers each interviewing 57 applicants for jobs as salesmen. It turned out that there was very little agreement between the interviewers in respect of how they rated the applicants; for example, a man rated first (i.e. the best applicant) by one interviewer was rated 57th (last) by another. This early investigation was somewhat crude, but its findings have, in general, been supported by many later studies. The fact that different interviewers assessing the same applicants can, and often do, come to widely different judgements of them clearly indicates that the interview as it is normally carried out is a highly unreliable way of selecting people.

* The second attempts to find how well interview judgements predict the actual job performance of the applicants selected. In other words, if you interview a number of people and select two, one of whom you think is barely acceptable but the other you rate as very good, does the one your interview assessment said was best really do the job better than the one you thought was a borderline case? This research on the validity of interview judgements unfortunately produces results no more comforting than the studies of agreement between interviewers. For example, an investigation to find out how well college interviews predicted final degree classification showed that as good (or perhaps, more appropriately, as bad) a result could have been achieved by simply picking the names and degree results out of a hat.

The unflattering picture of the value of interviewing as a means of assessment that has emerged from research has not, it would seem, dampened the enthusiasm for the technique. It remains the principal selection technique despite the many adverse findings. We shall see later that much can be done to improve the quality of interviewing and possibly even of the judgements arising from it, but it remains at present a rather imprecise way of assessing people. Why, then, do intelligent people who know about the fallibility of the interview persist in relying on it?

Why Interviews Are Still Used

There are a number of reasons why the interview retains its popularity:

* On purely pragmatic grounds, it is very easy to arrange and to carry out. (Unfortunately, it is all too easy to carry out *badly*, but not as easy to carry out well!)

* More important is the fact that an interview provides information that is difficult or impossible to obtain in other ways, e.g. what a candidate's appearance is like, how they conduct themselves in a face-to-face meeting, whether they express themselves clearly and well when speaking, whether they seem pleasant and personable, and so on.

* Applicants usually *prefer* to be seen; they dislike the impersonal approach of being assessed entirely 'on paper' as it were, and like to make some contact with the 'human face' of the organisation.

* Quite apart from vague subjective reactions, interviews present the opportunity for the candidate to ask questions about the job, conditions of employment and so forth.

* So both sides have a vested interest in the continued use of the interview, 'warts and all'.

How Interviewees Can Help Themselves

Most organisations have no intention of giving up the interview as a way of choosing people, though they will use all sorts of devices to train and assist their interviewers in the hope they will do a better job of assessing people. Where does this leave the interviewee? (N.B. Throughout this book, the term 'interviewee', 'candidate' and 'applicant' will be used interchangeably.) Must they just accept that the interview is an imperfect procedure and hope either that they are faced by a good interviewer or that they are just lucky that day? They certainly have to accept that the interview is imperfect, but they do not have to take a negative, helpless attitude towards their own role in it – quite the contrary. They should realise that, since even the most experienced interviewers sometimes make mistakes (precisely what sort of mistakes we will look at in Chapter 3), they cannot afford to take a totally passive role in the interview and it will often be up to them to make sure that their aptitudes, abilities and qualifications for the job are put forward and noted in the interview. To be in a position to do this, the candidate needs to know what kind of thing to expect in interviews, how to prepare in advance and how to deal with the interview situation itself.

The Aim of This Book

People attending for interviews are frequently unaware of what sort of questions are typically asked and of *why* the interviewer asks questions of that sort. The interviewees are rather like students having to take an exam where they know what the subject is but have never actually been told the syllabus. Small wonder that many of them come out of the interview feeling a mixture of bewilderment, resentment and regret – regret at the feeling they did not put themselves across better, that they have not done themselves justice. The aim of this book is to avoid situations of that kind; in other words, it sets out to help you put your best foot forward in the interview. It seeks to achieve this by doing basically two things:

* It describes how and why interviews are used, who carries them out, the different types of interviews likely to be encountered and the sort of questions asked. This should help remove some of the mystery and folklore that seem to shroud interviews and sometimes make people more nervous about them.

* It gives detailed and structured guidance on preparing for the interview, conduct and self-presentation in it and self-review after it. This information should enable you to take a more positive and active role in the interview itself. Quite apart from helping you personally, it should help the interviewer make better selection decisions (i.e. the decision as to who gets the job): if you have a better idea of what to expect in advance, how to prepare for it and tackle it, you should be able to put across more useful and valid information than would be the case if you were answering the questions hastily on the spur of the moment.

What This Book Will Not Do

This book does not give advice on how to 'trick' interviewers or on how to fake one's way through selection procedures. It is not intended to help an individual obtain a job irrespective of their merits for filling that job.

Whom the Book Is Meant for

The book has been written mainly with those leaving school or college and seeking their first full-time job in mind, particularly those who are going for jobs where educational qualifications will be of some importance. The reasons for limiting its aims in this way are:

* This group of interviewees need help on interviews more than most, because they have so little experience of them. As they attend more interviews, so their competence in handling them increases up to a point – but by that time several important job opportunities may

have been lost, never to return. The earlier this group can be given some help on interviews, the better.

* The kinds of interviews faced by this broad group of people are often fairly similar in many respects.

So what is contained in the following pages has been written with one specific (albeit large) group in mind. However, much of the information and advice given does in fact apply to interviews in general and is thus likely to be useful to many people outside the group I have mentioned. The other limitation on the content is that it does not address itself, except in passing, to the speculative application. This is where people are writing off to organisations on the chance that they have something to offer as opposed to responding to a specific advert.

The Way the Book Is Organised and How to Use It
Although we are chiefly concerned with the interview, two chapters have been devoted to consideration of the application form (Chapter 2) and the use of selection procedures other than the interview (e.g. psychological tests), which might be given along with it (Chapter 7). The rest of the book concentrates on the interview.

To really understand the interview and what goes on in it, you need to have a glimpse of what it looks like from the other side of the desk. Chapter 3 tries to show how the whole thing looks through the interviewer's eyes. Chapter 4 looks at the different types of interview and how they are conducted, then reviews the kind of questions interviewers ask and explains why they ask them. Following that we have the core of the book, which deals with how to prepare for the interview (Chapter 5) and how to conduct yourself in it (Chapter 6). The book ends with a chapter on reviewing your own performance in interviews (Chapter 8). Clearly most people will concentrate on what is said about preparing for and dealing with interviews, but do not skip the other chapters. You should read through the book once and then re-read Chapters 5 and 6. Shortly before the actual interview you will probably wish to use the Interview Preparation Programme and Checklist provided in Chapter 5, and shortly after the interview the last chapter should be re-read.

One final word. The idea for this book arose from my own experience as a practising psychologist; many of the interviewees I see have little idea of what seems to be expected of them and of how to deal with being interviewed. The information and advice given here rests largely on my experience as an interviewer, as a trainer of interviewers and (as will be seen in Chapter 6) on the results of a survey of other interviewers that I have conducted. It is also based on psychological research studies, where these are relevant. However, I have seldom made this research base explicit as to do so would probably turn this into a rather different and possibly less readable kind of book.

2

The First Step

Getting Your Name on the Shortlist
It is all very well talking about interviews and how to handle them, but there is the small matter of actually getting an interview in the first place. The first step usually involves filling in an application form or sending a curriculum vitae (CV); the latter is a brief outline of the main facts concerning your life to date. In either case, an accompanying letter of application may be asked for, and is probably desirable even if it is not requested. This chapter will offer some advice on how to put yourself across on paper and improve your chances of being called for an interview.

Most job adverts attract far more applicants than there are vacancies, particularly in times of high unemployment. This gives the employing organisation a bit of a problem. With numerous applications to work through they could spend a ridiculous length of time arriving at a shortlist of the few best applicants. In order to reduce this task to manageable proportions, the usual practice is to sift through them all and reject those that appear to be of lesser quality when judged on some basic standard. For example, if a job requires that the job-holder should have a good degree, then whoever is sifting the applications may start by simply picking out the applicants who have the best degrees of this particular bunch, and rejecting the rest; then they would go through the others in more detail before drawing up a final shortlist for interview. This first sift of applications is often a rather arbitrary procedure; an application can even be dismissed at this stage on the grounds of being untidy or difficult to read. So you cannot afford to be careless in the way you tackle it.

The Curriculum Vitae

The CV seems more difficult to deal with than an application form in some respects, mainly because when CVs are asked for it is seldom specified just what they should contain. In fact, putting a CV together is reasonably straightforward, particularly if you have little work experience to describe. An illustration of the kind of lay-out often used is given in Example 1. However, since almost everything we would want to say about writing CVs we would also want to say in connection with filling out application forms, we will move on to the latter topic without further ado. Just remember that what follows applies equally to CVs.

The Application Form

Two main concerns are that the form be filled in neatly and *correctly*. To achieve this:

* Read through the form carefully before writing anything on it.

* Then, on a separate piece of paper, write out the information you are going to put under each section of the form; this will often bring any errors or uncertainties to light and prevent you having to cross things out on the form itself. This 'practice' element is particularly important if the form has sections on it which require you to compose some paragraphs – for example, some forms ask you to write a short autobiographical sketch, or to list all the key events in your life and say why they are important.

EXAMPLE 1

CV

John Smith
139 Bowring Park Road, Liverpool L14 6NW
Telephone 051-439 1215

Date of Birth: 31 July 1960 : Age 26

Education
Quarry Bank Comprehensive   1971–78
Sheffield University   1978–81
Polytechnic of Central London 1982–84

Qualifications
A levels in English (B), History (C), Geography (D) (1978)
BA Honours Degree (2:2) in English (1981)
Diploma in Management Studies (1984)

Work Experience
Executive Officer, Department of the Environment, London, 1981–84

Worked in a section dealing with Public Enquiries into proposals for new motorways. My responsibilities included supervising two clerical staff, taking minutes of meetings, preparing of drafts, liaising with local authority representatives, handling queries from members of the general public. Completed DMS course part-time while in this job. Left to get experience in the private sector and to obtain a post with greater personal responsibility.

Assistant Manager, Rutherford Export Ltd, London 1984–date

Working in an export company offices on arrangements for dispatch of orders by sea. Responsibilities include supervising four clerical and secretarial staff, negotiating contract terms with shipping companies, overseeing the arrangements for the company's move to new offices, and deputising for the manager on various occasions. Present salary: £9,800.

Interests
Football (captained 1st XI at University), Reading, Amateur Dramatics

Other Information
Clean driving licence
Health excellent

References

* Having written things out in rough, give yourself a day or so and then come back to it, look through it all again and, if it still makes sense, copy it out on to the application form itself. Better still, get it *typed* on the form if you can; this looks a lot neater and is easier to read. If you cannot get it typed, then make sure you write it as neatly as possible. Should your writing not be very legible, try printing your answers where appropriate.

* When you have completed it, read through the finished form. Check that all the information asked for is provided and that the spelling is correct (both of which should be right if you have given some thought to these matters in the first drafting stage). Also, check the dates given, for instance in relation to a series of starting and leaving dates for jobs or schools; are there any inconsistencies or unexplained gaps?

Most of what has been said so far relates to the presentation of the form, which is particularly important in reducing the danger of being disqualified at the preliminary sifting stage.

The most important thing, however, is obviously the content of the application. When writing a first draft as suggested above, think about what you are saying and try to look at it from the point of view of the organisation to which you are applying: how will the information given on the form be interpreted and what are the sort of things looked for?

In this context, do not make the mistake of thinking that any vacation or temporary work you have done is too brief or menial to be mentioned. Having been active and gainfully employed is something that is worth letting people know. And it may say quite a lot about you. For instance, if you have worked at the same place two or three vacations running, it implies that you were seen as a reliable worker who they are glad to have back. Or if you have survived for some weeks in a job that has quite a bit of pressure – like being a waitress in a busy restaurant – it suggests that you are not going to buckle at the knees the first time some demands are made on you.

Whatever the job, be it permanent or temporary, you should look at your time in it and consider what experience and knowledge it gave you. Quite apart from then being able to talk about it more impressively in an interview if you are asked, an analysis of what you got out of the job may help you get clear in your mind what it is that you havè to offer an employer. Certainly, any achievement, mark of recognition (like a promotion, or an extension of your responsibilities) or skill acquired should be mentioned on the form.

One of the best ways to present this kind of information is to try using lots of 'action' words:

● Achieved

● Set up

● Directed

● Devised

● Wrote

● Elected

● Started

● Supervised

● Organised

● Prepared

● Initiated

● Planned

There are many more, of course. If you can describe your work experience, in part, by sentences beginning with words of this kind, it will not only help you to avoid saying 'I' all the time – which does not read well – but make the whole thing sound more dynamic. There is an element of this in Example 1, though it could have been developed further.

One other point about listing work experience – sometimes it is presented in reverse order, with the most recent or present job first. There is no hard and fast rule on this, though if you have been through a lot of jobs it probably does help whoever is reading the form to get clear from the context just what your present position is. The application forms usually make it clear which order to list your jobs in anyway.

As has already been implied, the context of the form generally plays some part in deciding what will be talked about in the interview. So what you put down now, say in regard to your leisure interests (see pp. 46–7 and 60–1 in this connection), you may well have to discuss in more detail if you are given an interview. *Do* put down things you will be happy to enlarge on orally and *avoid* putting down things that you will have difficulty talking about (unless, of course, they have to be mentioned, such as jobs you were not good at but which have to be included in your employment history). Try to ensure that anything that might work in your favour is included – all exam passes, extra qualifications, sporting or other achievements, social or community work, special projects, and so on. If the form provides only very limited space for you to give information of certain kinds, then make sure that the information most relevant to that job is included, even if there is little or no room for anything else. For example, if the job was in the area of social services, and you had done some voluntary work helping old people, it would make sense to give that prominence.

Finally!
Keep you first 'rough' draft of the application form or (preferably) photocopy it. Then, if you get an interview you will be able to refresh your memory of what you wrote on it and think about the kinds of questions that are likely to arise from that.

References

You will usually be asked, somewhere on the form, to give the names and addresses of people who will give you a reference (two are generally asked for). These referees may just be people who know you well and will vouch for your 'good character', or they may have to be people who have some knowledge of your ability and achievements shown in employment or education.

Irrespective of which kind of referee is required, always contact them and seek their consent before you put their name down on an application form. Many people would be willing to act as referees but take mild offence (or worse) at having this fact taken for granted. Not only is it polite to ask, but you can at the same time tell them about the job you are applying for. Taking this further, you might suggest what things could be stressed in the reference that would help this particular application – but whether or not you go as far as this very much depends on how well you know, and get on with, your referee.

It is quite good politics to write to the people you ask references of even when you are not applying for jobs. Letting them know what you are doing and how you are getting on occasionally will make them feel much happier about providing references when the time comes; they are less likely to feel that you are just making a convenience of them. This is important, as writing a well-worded reference takes time, and if they have to do it repeatedly for you your referees need all the 'encouragement' you can give them (and that includes letting them know afterwards whether or not you got the job, and thanking them for their help either way).

WHO TO NAME AS REFEREES

Many people find they have little choice anyway, as there are only one or two people who can really comment on their performance at college or at work. If you are lucky, however, you might have the choice of several people open to you; this happens more and more as you get older, because you work with a greater variety of people over time. The main points to keep in mind when deciding who to ask are:

* How much prestige or influence do they have?

* How well do they know your work and abilities?

* How well do you get on with them?

* How relevant is their knowledge of you to *this* application?

The above points are *not* listed in priority; it is up to you to decide your own priorities on this.

One problem that frequently arises is that you do not wish to give your present employer as a referee when applying for a job, lest the knowledge that you are looking around for something else should jeopardise your present position. If other referees are available, then this can obviously be dealt with. However, if you have had only one job, the problem remains. In such a case, it is probably best to ring the organisation you are applying to and ask them whether or not they would be willing to defer writing to your employer until after the interview (references are usually taken up only when a candidate is shortlisted for interview). Then, if you have not got the job they will not bother to write, and if you have been provisionally accepted your employer will probably have the good grace to accept the situation. (Even if they do not, and write a bad reference, it is unlikely to lead to a reversal of the interview decision.) Clearly, there is an element of risk in this strategy and you must balance this against whatever level of risk you see in admitting to your employer beforehand that you are looking for other jobs and asking for a reference: the reaction to the latter is not always negative, and sometimes even produces incentives to stay!

The Letter of Application
It is relatively rare these days to be asked to make your application in the form of a letter. More often, you just

need to write a letter to accompany the application form or CV which gives the pertinent information, and that is the context in which it will be looked at here.

Where you have had to fill in an application form, the covering letter can be brief. The people on the receiving end will probably have more than enough to read anyway and will not thank you for taking up any more of their time than is necessary. In these circumstances, your letter will simply be a gesture of politeness as much as anything, though it might also serve as a way of quickly identifying which job your application relates to.

There may be occasions, however, when you need to impart some other information that you feel is relevant but that the application form does not give you scope to convey. If this is the case, the additional material can be included in your covering letter. This is illustrated in Example 2; take a look at it now and spot the ways in which it needs to be improved.

EXAMPLE 2

The Personnel Manager   The Laurels
BSRD Products   74 St James' Drive
Kirkland House   London SW11
North Road
Cardiff

Dear Sir
I am in the third and final year of my sociology degree course at Middlesex University and I am interested in your advertisement for the post of management trainee. I enclose my completed application form for this job. As you will see, I have covered a number of options in my course that are relevant to management generally. I should also add that I speak fluent German and also perhaps explain that the year I spent out of college (1984–85) was due to family problems.

Yours Sincerely

N. O. Hope

There are quite a few things wrong with N. O. Hope's letter:

- the letter is undated
- no telephone number is given
- no postcodes are quoted; if you know them, put them down – it can speed up delivery
- usually, job adverts carry a reference number, which should be included in your letter; N. O. Hope has omitted it
- the letter assumes the Personnel Manager to be male
- instead of getting to the point quickly, the letter begins by repeating information already in the application form
- in the sentence commencing 'As you will see', the letter again just repeats what is in the form
- when important additional information is given (on the year spent out of college), it is left too vague
- having opened with 'Dear Sir', the letter should end with 'Yours faithfully'!
- the letter is poorly organised all round.

Example 3 illustrates a much better covering letter.

Writing a covering letter to go with a CV as opposed to an application form requires a little more, both in content and in thought. Since the CV simply presents a set of facts about who you are and what you have done, the accompanying letter might usefully include some statement as to *why* you want this particular job. In addition, it can present any other information that you think is relevant to your application but that is not obvious from the CV itself.

PRESENTATION
The comments made earlier about the importance of good presentation of application forms apply just as forcibly to letters.

EXAMPLE 3

Mr G Hunt
Personnel officer
FDA Ltd
100 Prince of Wales Drive
London SW11 8IT

125 Clairville Road
Bromley
Kent BR6 9SD
(Tel. 01-388 7812)

19 February 1986

Your reference ST1/86/2/16

Dear Mr Hunt

I enclose my completed application form for the post of Administrative Assistant in FDA Ltd. While I am sure this will provide you with most of the relevant details, there is one further piece of information that perhaps should be added and which does not come up under any of the form's headings. You will see that I took a year off between leaving school and going to University. This was a consequence of my mother becoming seriously ill shortly after my 'A' levels. I had to then stay at home to help look after my three younger brothers and sisters until my mother recovered, which was almost a year later. I was determined to go to college and did as much reading for my course in that period as circumstances allowed, which no doubt helped me get my place at Bristol University.

Yours sincerely

(Miss) Caroline Egan

---

* They should be written (or typed) on plain white paper of reasonable quality – pink 'n' perfumed is definitely out!

* Express yourself in a straightforward, business-like fashion and do not indulge in fancy phrases like 'with reference to your advertisement of the 21st inst', or 'it is with pleasure that I enclose my application for . . .'.

* Once again, check your spelling and grammar, and take a copy of the letter.

* Finally, print your name under your signature if there is the faintest chance that it may be difficult to read.

Summary of Advice

☞ Make a draft of what you want to write (for letters, CVs, or application forms) on a separate piece of paper first.

☞ Emphasise the most relevant and positive aspects of your qualifications and experience.

☞ Give yourself time to think over your first draft before writing the final version.

☞ Make sure that your form/CV/letter of application is presented neatly; get it typed if possible.

☞ Read through and check for errors (spelling, grammar, dates out of sequence, etc.).

☞ Keep covering letters of application short and to the point; avoid repetition of what is on the form or CV.

☞ Keep a copy of what you sent.

☞ Choose your referees with care.

☞ Consult any people you are thinking of as referees and get their permission first.

☞ Thank them and inform them of the outcome of your application afterwards.

3

Interviewers: Their Task and Problems

The aim of this chapter is to put you in the other person's shoes, to see how things look from the interviewer's side of the desk. Some of the apprehension people feel about interviews springs from knowing so little about them as a procedure. In the following pages we will look at who does the interviewing, the basic task that confronts interviewers and the problems involved. This should not only take away some of the mystery from interviews but also make you a little more confident about facing them.

Who Carries out the Interview?

The person you face in an interview may be there through accident or design. They may have been selected almost randomly to carry out the interview or they may have been carefully chosen because of their knowledge of the job that is vacant and of the kinds of skills that will be needed by whoever fills it. One thing is almost certain: the interviewers will not be chosen because they have a gift for assessing people; if such individuals exist, they are seldom seen in interviews. So he or she will be a fairly average mortal, a fact easily lost sight of (sometimes by both parties) in the interview itself. Most commonly the interviewer is either someone from the personnel department or is the person who will be responsible for the work of whoever is to be appointed. In larger organisations, which tend to spend more time and money on selecting people for jobs, the candidate may be interviewed by representatives of both personnel and line management functions. There is some research showing that personnel managers look for slightly different things in job applicants compared to what other kinds of managers seem to concentrate on, but these differences are not large enough to be worth worrying about.

If you are going for a really important job, the organisation may even unleash a psychologist as well as the other interviewers on you! Most people find that a relatively painless experience, I should hasten to add.

The ability to judge others

Trying to assess the personality of another person on the basis of a brief meeting, like an interview, is extremely difficult. We have already seen (in Chapter 1) how different interviewers often come to widely different judgements about the same applicant. Our assessments of other people are influenced by many things, some of them quite irrelevant. A lot of psychological research in the 1950s was aimed at establishing what were the characteristics of individuals who were good at judging other people. Some people were found to be better than others at gauging the character and temperament of certain groups of people (e.g. students, middle-class housewives, etc.), particularly if they themselves were members of the same group – but the search for a type of person who is good at making personality assessments of other people in general was unsuccessful.

Experienced interviewers

Some interviewers find it hard to accept that simply doing more interviews does not of itself make them better at judging others (a fact established by research). After all, most of us like to feel that we can get the measure of somebody given a reasonable chance to chat with them, and if you are doing this kind of thing all the time (in the form of interviews) there is an understandable tendency to think that you are pretty good at assessing others. This occasionally gets taken to extremes by interviewers who claim that they can 'sum a man up as soon as he walks in the room'. Such claims tell us more about the person making them than they do about the interviewees, but fortunately one does not encounter that kind of ill-found arrogance very often.

If the amount of interviewing they have done makes no difference to their basic ability to assess people, do experienced interviewers have anything else going for them? Well, experienced interviewers are usually more confident and have a better idea of what questions they want to ask – the result being an interview that moves along more comfortably for both sides and that will probably yield more information than an interview given by an inexperienced person. Unfortunately, without proper training there is quite a chance that the information obtained will be irrelevant to the selection process; and even with such training and useful information elicited in the interview, there is no guarantee that an experienced interviewer will actually *use* the information better in making a decision on who to appoint.

Inexperienced interviewers

Inexperienced interviewers are usually easy enough to spot. Their lack of confidence shows in stammering, hesitancy and other aspects of the way they put their questions. Sometimes they bravely try to cover up with excessive casualness – like one interviewer I heard ask a candidate 'Are you married at all?' To which the candidate would have been justified (but unwise) in replying 'Only a bit' or 'Yes, sometimes'. Quite often they dry up in the middle of an interview because they have not prepared properly or simply cannot think of what to ask next. This nervousness has an unsettling effect on some interviewees, and they lose confidence too, though some seem to relish the situation and more or less take control of the interview. However, generally speaking you are better off in the hands of an experienced interviewer, particularly one who has been properly trained.

The interviewer as a public relations officer

An organisation will of course shortlist for interview quite a few more applicants than it has vacant jobs. So for every 100 people taken on, maybe 300–400 will be rejected following an interview. This may be the only time that those rejected applicants will have face-to-face contact with a representative of that organisation. If the interview was badly conducted, or seemed unfair, or if the interviewer treated the applicant less than politely, then the rejection will just add insult to injury. Any organisation that is conscious of its public image will want to avoid that situation – it does not want a lot of disgruntled interviewees going round giving it a bad name. So interviewers, if they are any good, will always be conscious of their public relations role and act accordingly (though this is not much more than they should do through good manners anyway). This is also a point that the employing organisation should keep in mind when choosing who to do the interviewing for it.

Matching People and Jobs

It would be impossible to select people for jobs effectively without knowing a good deal about the jobs themselves. A thorough description of the job, the duties it involves and the circumstances under which it has to be done is required. When this information is available, in the form of a **job specification,** one can start thinking about the kind of abilities, qualities and experience that will be required to do it properly. This may lead to an idea of what an ideal candidate might be like. It is highly unlikely that any candidate will be wholly ideal, so there should be a list of priorities giving the most important and the least important (i.e. those that are essential and those that are just desirable) of the qualities wanted, which will help decide which of the job applicants seems the most suitable.

Job specifications are very useful for getting clear in interviewers' minds just what it is they are looking for. However, sometimes it is difficult to draw up a precise specification because people are being recruited to a general group of jobs, for example, executive officers in the Civil Service might be called upon to perform a variety of very different tasks at various stages in their career. Similarly, graduate management trainees entering large organisations are often given experience of numerous kinds of work before settling down to one main field. In these instances, the job specification will be expressed in much more general terms and selection will probably rely heavily on academic qualifications and the candidates' ability to convey a favourable impression of their personality in the interview. The interviewers are looking more for potential rather than an existing set of skills, which makes their task considerably harder.

So, with varying degrees of precision, the interviewers will know what information they need to get from applicants to assess their suitability for the job as specified. We shall see in Chapter 4 how they go about collecting that information and the kind of interview plans they use. All that we need to note here is that they will use a number of different sources of information, including references, academic qualifications, work experience and performance in the interview.

The matching process is a two-way affair in most cases; the applicants for a job will be seeking further information about it in the interview to make sure it is broadly what they thought it was and thus suitable for them. Quite often applicants find out things about the job in the interview that lead them to reject it when offered. This opportunity for the candidate to get further details and check on terms, etc., is an important part of the selection process and emphasises again that interviewees should not be thought of as passive elements in the selection situation. However, most applicants do decide they want the job and so the final decision rests with the interviewer. How do they make up their mind? If they have carried out their task properly, they should have on the one hand a job specification telling them what they need, and on the other an assessment of each of the applicants they have seen on those attributes required. They then have to match the two sides together and see who fits the job specification most closely. That might seem simple, but is often anything but easy. For example, if the job specification lists three qualities or qualifications A, B and C in order of priority, the interviewer may find at the end of the day that there is one candidate who was excellent on A and moderate on B and C, another who was excellent on B and C but only moderate on A, and a third who was good, but not excellent, on all three. Which would they choose? Under such circumstances all sorts of personal factors might tip the balance in favour of one of the three, but the main point is that even with a systematic approach to selecting people the final decision does not get reduced to a mathematical exercise – the decision is often extremely difficult and influenced by all sorts of factors, both relevant and irrelevant. We shall look at some of them later in the next section.

The Problems Involved

Carrying out a good interview is far from easy; carrying out a bad one is all too easy. In this section we shall look at the kind of problems interviewers have to deal with and overcome if they are to do their job properly. A knowledge of these problems should help you understand what goes on in the interview and give you a better chance of dealing with it. It might even make you more sympathetic toward the interviewers!

The constraints on the interview

Time is the most obvious constraint; in most selection procedures several or all of the applicants have to be seen on one day, with each allotted a fixed time period. So the interviewers are generally working against the clock, which makes it all the more imperative that they use that limited amount of time to the maximum effect. Good interviewers will have worked out in advance the sort of things they want to talk about and will have planned the interview time accordingly. The less effective ones will frequently run out of time when they have covered only half of what they intended or, in some cases, will dry up half way through the interview.

A very different and fundamental constraint on the interview is that there is relatively little one can do to find out whether or not the interviewee is being **truthful.** Paper qualifications, etc., can be checked, and references may provide further evidence on some things, but most of the other information has to be taken on trust from the interviewee. Skilful interviewing and observation of the interviewee's behaviour will often reveal some exaggerations or even downright lies (e.g. when someone claims to have a deep knowledge of a particular subject and when questioned on it appears to know little or nothing), but a great deal of what is said by interviewees remains unverifiable. This is something an interviewer just has to live with.

Getting the interviewee to talk freely

Even people who are confident and self-assured at other times can be nervous when being interviewed, and this presents interviewers with one of their most common problems. The trouble is that when someone is tense, they tend to say less, to be hesitant in answering, to be less open about themselves and generally to be less communicative (although there are some who react the other way by talking all the time as a way of trying to stop the interviewer from asking questions). This is bad from the interviewee's standpoint because they feel uncomfortable and give a poor impression, while the interviewer finds out little more about the interviewee than the fact that they are nervous in interviews. Some people might say 'Well, fair enough – they cannot face pressure so we will not employ them'. That, however, is a dangerous line of reasoning. A whole career may depend on an interview, and there are not many more important (and thus possibly anxiety-provoking) occasions than that; certainly everyday work situations seldom generate anything nearly as important to the individual, and nothing that they will get quite so charged-up about. So reactions to being interviewed should not be taken as altogether typical of how the individual faces stressful situations. And even if it is, interviewers should ask themselves whether the successful applicant will really be doing a job in which coping with stress is important anyway.

Bias

Why is it that different interviewers seeing the same person so often come to different assessments of that person (as in the study of salesmen mentioned in Chapter 1)? It could be that they started out with different ideas of what they were looking for, or that they asked different questions. Often, however, the reason for such varying assessment can come down to fairly simple old-fashioned prejudice or bias. We all have biases of some sort – things about other people that set our teeth on edge. Interviewers are no exception. Some of the things I have heard interviewers say they found objectionable about applicants include biting fingernails, chewing gum, chain smoking, not looking you in the eye, shifting in the chair too often, making too many hand gestures, fiddling with pens or other objects in their hands, tapping feet.

Quite a few of these are clearly unreasonable things to hold against somebody, particularly in the context of an interview. But biases are not necessarily rational – one interviewer disliked candidates who had 'short arms' or acne! Indeed, it is all too common to find that people have prejudices based on physical characteristics. What can be done to offset the effects of such biases – which are after all irrelevant to the job (except possibly where the successful candidate is going to be working closely with the interviewer)? Unfortunately, very little. The important thing is that interviewers be aware of this danger and, through training or otherwise, identify their own particular biases. Even then, research has suggested that this does not always stop those biases operating.

From the *interviewee's* standpoint, the only way of not falling foul of interviewers' biases is to look at the examples cited earlier and try to avoid doing those sorts of things in interviews. However, more of that in Chapter 6. For the moment it is sufficient to note that personality judgements generally are fraught with difficulty and subject to many distorting influences. I have mentioned here just two that are of particular importance in the interview, but there are numerous others.

Other pitfalls of interviewing
One study of interviewers selecting personnel for the Canadian armed forces showed that the majority of the interviewers were, in effect, making their minds up about candidates within the first four minutes of the interview. This in itself is bad enough, as not only was there insufficient time to gather adequate information on which to base a decision, but the interviewers were often making their judgements on irrelevant information as well. However, the interviewers in this study seemed to form an initial impression of the candidate and then sought information that was consistent with that initial impression. Other investigations have thrown up the same kind of observation, i.e. that interviewers decide to accept or reject the candidate early in the interview and then – largely unconsciously in all probability – conduct the rest of the session in such a way that they collect or perceive only that information that supports the judgement they have already made. The danger of making up one's mind about an applicant very early in an interview, and of the whole thing then becoming a self-fulfilling prophecy, is very real. As Dr Johnson said, 'God Himself, Sir, does not presume to

judge a man until the end of his days.' As mere mortals, interviewers should have the decency and humility to wait to the end of the interview before judging an applicant. Fortunately, quite a lot of them do.

The commonest pitfall of interviewing is the poor phrasing of questions. Much of what interviewers get out of candidates depends on their asking the right type of questions. If they use 'closed' questions, i.e. questions that simply require 'yes' or 'no' or other equally brief answers, they will take a long time to get a little information. One often hears this type of question combined with the unfortunate and time-wasting habit of reading the application form to the candidate at the beginning of an interview:

'You went to X school?' – 'Yes'
'And you got Z qualifications there?' – 'Yes'
'After that you went to Y college?' – 'That's right'

Closed questions are inevitable sometimes and they do have their place, for example with candidates who are very unresponsive and despite encouragement offer little information about themselves. In such instances, a lot of closed questions might have to be asked. This is getting information the hard way. I fondly remember one interviewer who had to talk to a candidate about her leisure interests. Unfortunately for him, the candidate was a girl of 19 whose only interest was motor-cycles. The interviewer, knowing nothing about motor-bikes or the culture associated with them, desperately tried every interest he could think of to try to get something to talk about, culminating in the ludicrously unlikely closed question:

'Do you ever get together as a family and play Ludo?'

Interviewers should try to use open-ended questions that afford the candidate the opportunity to say a lot more than just 'yes' or 'no' in reply. So, instead of asking

'Did you join the dramatic society at college?'

they should ask

> 'How did you spend your leisure time when you were at college?'

– or something along those lines. The whole point of such questions refers back to the problem mentioned earlier of getting people to talk in the interview. When they do answer at some length, they will often produce leads that the interviewer can follow up with narrower, more detailed questions.

Another mistake interviewers are prone to make is to ask leading questions, i.e. those that give the interviewee a clear indication of the answer they should give. Sometimes this is quite blatant:

> 'This job calls for the ability to plan; do you like planning?'

to which any candidate in their right mind will answer 'Yes'. On other occasions, the leading question betrays the interviewer's own beliefs and expectancies with varying degrees of subtlety, like the senior public servant I heard ask of a candidate

> 'What do you think of the way the President has been pilloried by the Press over this affair?'

There are numerous other mistakes one can all too easily make in phrasing interview questions, and we shall see more of them in Chapter 6 when we consider the best ways of dealing with each type.

Interpreting and using the information obtained
When interviewers have grappled with all these problems, with varying success, they come up against what is the final and possibly the biggest problem: how to use the information they obtained to make a (hopefully, correct) decision. They have some factual information on the candidates, and a great deal of subjective information based on their interview impressions.

This will all vary in terms of its relevance and importance to the task of accepting or rejecting people. Part
of the problem is that any interview conducted reasonably well can provide the interviewer with too
much data. All human beings have limited information-
processing capacity; that is, they can use only certain
limited amounts of information to any effect over a
given period. Trying to itemise all the information
obtained, weigh it up and combine it to come to a
selection decision probably is too big a task for our
information-processing capacity to handle. A look at
the complex research on this aspect of interviewing is
beyond the scope of this book, but, in general, it shows
that interviewers have to over-simplify the decision
process as a way of keeping the task manageable. This
involves all sorts of things, like sometimes giving much
more weight to anything negative about the interviewee than to anything positive, using only part of the
information available (which is what we see when
interviewers make up their minds too quickly) and so
on.

THE INTERVIEWER AS FORTUNE TELLER

Quite apart from the strategies interviewers employ –
largely unconsciously it should be said – to arrive at a
decision, there is the immense difficulty inherent in the
nature of the decision or judgement they have to make.
In effect, they are trying to predict the future. They are
being asked to say whether the individual they have
briefly met will be able to take on at a later date a set of
duties and perform them well. Not only that, but they
are often required to pick people who have potential for
development, who are going to be capable of doing
many more senior jobs in time to come. When one
remembers how much people and circumstances
change over time, the difficulty of the interviewer's
task is clear. All they have to go on is the impression
they have of the candidates as they are here and now,
and a past record of educational or other achievement.
Neither past nor present performance is a particularly

good indicator of how well people will perform at higher levels in the future.

So both the process of coming to a decision on selecting an applicant and the kind of judgement being made in that decision present great difficulties for interviewers. If they have tried as hard as they can to carry out their task well, they deserve your understanding of their problems, even if you do not always agree with the decisions they make!

And just in case you think that this is all an excuse to cover up for the mistakes interviewers make, here is some cold comfort for you. The decisions doctors make are subject to the same kind of information-processing limitations as those of the personnel interviewers, with rather similar results. For example, one study had an experienced group of medical practitioners examine stomach X-rays of patients with gastric ulcers and decide in each case whether the ulcer was benign or malignant. Broadly speaking, there are seven major signs that can be looked for in an X-ray to help make this particular diagnosis, and these signs are related to each other in a complex way that should be taken account of in making the diagnosis. The study revealed that the doctors just could not handle the complexity of this decision task and that they simplified it in much the same way as interviewers do. No doubt partly as a consequence of this, the doctors often disagreed with one another in their diagnosis. This is no isolated finding; there is plenty of other evidence (for example, the fact that around 80 per cent of appendectomies are found to be unnecessary) to point to the difficulty medical practitioners have in making decisions even on the basis of relatively objective evidence.

Personnel interviewers, working with little objective evidence and a great deal of subjective impression, have an even harder task; but at least they have the comfort of knowing that their mistakes are unlikely to kill anyone!

What You and the Interviewer Are Entitled to Expect
When talking to people after they have come out of interviews it is apparent that many of them have little or a wrong idea of what they were supposed to expect. Some have the idea that they are supposed to be treated like glass – fragile, handle with care – while others expect various degrees of interrogation up to a level not far short of the Inquisition. As a rough guide, you are entitled to expect the following:

- that you will be treated with courtesy

- that you will be given adequate opportunity to say what you want and that the interviewer will listen attentively

- that both your good points and your defects will be noted and taken into account providing they are judged relevant

- that you will be made to think hard and (often) quickly at some stages in the interview, e.g. when having to defend your viewpoint on a topic

- that the interviewer will withhold judgement on your application until the end of the interview

- that the interviewer will base his assessment of your suitability on information relevant to the performance of the job in question.

In return, what is the interviewer entitled to expect of you? Basically that:

- you are serious in your application and thus about the interview itself

- you will be honest in your answers to any questions (providing they are fair), always allowing for some understandable distortions that creep in when people are talking about themselves

● you will be courteous and attentive

● you will be able to talk about anything you have indicated as being of special interest to you.

This does *not* extend as far as the case of one interviewer I remember. He was questioning a candidate who had seven years previously taken a fairly basic exam in economic and social history, which he used as justification to launch the following blockbuster: 'How does Britain's joining the European Economic Community fit in with her social and economic development over, say, the last 250 years?' This is an essay question rather than an interview question and was totally unjustified – all the more so as the interviewer could not even answer the question himself, as I made a point of finding out!

4

The Way Interviews are Conducted

Different Types of Interview

There are two main types of interview used in selection, the one-to-one interview and the panel interview. Both may be encountered in the same selection procedure, particularly in the more extended and sophisticated examples of such procedures. So you may be given a one-to-one interview first (as when employers visit the universities in the Spring each year on the so-called 'milk round'), which leads on later – if you make a good impression – to further sessions involving interviews of both types and possibly also some psychological tests. However, most organisations tend to use one type or the other, and do not mix them together in this way.

The one-to-one interview

This may also be called the individual interview, and as its name implies it consists simply of one interviewer talking with one applicant. It is the easiest interview to arrange and conduct, and in consequence is the type most commonly encountered. In particular, it is widely used in industry and commerce.

The individual interview has a number of advantages:

* It is relatively inexpensive to carry out in terms of man-hours.

* It is generally felt to be a more relaxed approach that moves away from the tense formality often associated with panel interviews and instead becomes more like a guided conversation between two people.

* If the interviewer is himself the person who will be supervising the work of the successful applicant, then both parties have an opportunity in the interview to size each other up and try to assess how well they would get on together (additionally, in this situation, the interviewer is particularly well-placed to answer the candidate's questions about what the job involves).

There are disadvantages to interviews of this kind, however:

* The main one is that it inevitably depends heavily on the personality and ability of one individual. If he is not a good interviewer, he may elicit the wrong kind of information, or perhaps very little information at all. Worse still, his own particular biases may determine who gets the job (though if the person who gets the post *is* going to have to work with him, it could be argued that for the sake of harmony this would be no bad thing).

* In the case of more general posts where the individual may get moved around from one part of the company to another fairly often in the early stages, one interviewer may not be in a position to give a full picture of the work and answer all the questions on it.

In order to overcome some of these disadvantages, many of the larger organisations carry out sequential interviews, i.e. a series of individual interviews. The different interviewers may cover different topic areas in the interviews (if they do not, they are duplicating each other's efforts), and between them should be able to represent the interests of the various sections of the organisation. With several interviewers pooling their judgements on a candidate, there should be less chance of the final decision being influenced by the particular prejudice of just one person.

The panel interview
Panel interviews are often referred to as board interviews. The panel or selection board may range from two to (in some absurd instances) 100 people, but usually consists of three to five interviewers who see the candidate together. This technique is particularly prevalent in public-sector bodies, such as the Civil Service, education authorities and so on.

The advantages of this kind of interview tend to be the opposite of the individual interview (i.e. the advantages of one are the disadvantages of the other, and vice versa):

* With a number of people carrying out the interview there is less chance of the applicant being treated unfairly as a result of a single interviewer's particular likes and dislikes; each interviewer acts as a check on the others' judgement and the procedure as a whole is fairer. Though a cynic might suggest that four interviewers just means four times as many prejudices and an even greater likelihood of rejection on irrelevant grounds, the board interview probably does help control much bias and moderate extreme views (if conducted properly) and thus is clearly of particular importance for posts in public service.

* The panel interview allows for division of labour amongst its members: each member can concentrate on a different topic.

* It also means that while one member of the board is talking with the applicant, the others will be listening

carefully for leads they can follow up when it is their turn to question him.

The biggest single drawback to this approach is that it is difficult to establish rapport; facing a row of four or five people sitting the other side of the table is not particularly conducive to feelings of calmness and relaxation. So the panel interview tends to be a rather formal procedure. Some applicants actually prefer this and feel more at ease with the more formal situation, but one feels the majority do not. The less rapport one can establish with an applicant, the less easy it is to get him to talk freely in an interview.

As in any interview, the individual's reaction to a panel interview depends in part on how it is conducted. If it is done well, the panel members will normally take it in turns to ask their questions of the candidate, and they will have agreed in advance what areas each one will cover. The first member may spend ten minutes questioning the applicants about their present and past jobs, the next one may spend a similar amount of time on education and qualifications, and so on. The alternative is a free for all in which any member of the board can ask questions at any time. This bombardment of questions coming in from different directions is apt to be rather confusing for the candidates, and does nothing to help them relax. It is also an inefficient method since at the end of sessions conducted in this manner the panel members usually find a collection of topics they have failed to raise.

The key figure of an interview board is the chairperson. He or she has the job of organising the board and its way of operating – often allocating the topics to be covered to the individual members of the panel, making sure that they do not overrun their time 'slots' during the interview, acting as a link between each member as one completes his questioning and another starts, and taking charge of the overall assessment of the candidate after the interview. The chairperson will normally be the first person to greet candidates when they enter the room and will probably ask the first few questions: it is their task to help the candidate settle down as quickly as possible. At the end of the interview, the chairperson will probably round off by asking a few supplementary questions (often ones that their colleagues have missed, or ones that arise from the candidate's previous replies), and then terminate the interview. Obviously, much will depend on how efficiently the chairperson controls the colleagues on the board; if they do it well, all will progress reasonably smoothly, but if they do not, a very awkward shambles of an interview will result.

A Systematic Approach – Sometimes

Having looked at the two main types of interview, we can turn to the way the interviews are conducted. One of the best ways of improving the standard of interviewing is to adopt a systematic approach – an interview *plan*. This does not mean that interviewers work out in detail everything they are going to ask beforehand and then plough through the list in the interview itself. All that is required in a planned approach is that they establish in advance what information is needed, how it can be organised under different headings and in what order and style those headings are going to be used to direct the progress of the interview. There are a number of such plans in common use, probably the best known being Professor Alec Rodger's 'Seven-Point Plan'. Typically, the information to be sought might be classified under the headings of present job, education and training, previous work history, interests, and family background. The order in which these topic areas are to be tackled in the interview, and what things are to be covered in them, should also be decided in advance, though in these respects the interviewer has to keep a degree of flexibility, so as to cope adequately with the inevitable variations between individual cases.

Most trained interviewers will work to a plan. The candidate may view this with mixed feelings. On the one hand, the kinds of things discussed in the interview will probably be easier to predict if a plan is being used, and the interviewer should cover all the relevant ground (so the candidate should have no complaint about important experience or attributes being ignored). On the other hand, if the interviewer is using a plan well, the interview will be a thoroughly testing one for the candidate – no easy ride!

This kind of systematic approach is still found only in a minority of cases – though an important minority, as it includes most of the interviews done for management trainee posts in the Civil Service and in large industrial organisations. The bulk of employment interviews continue to be done in rather haphazard fashion, the interviewers not having much idea of how they are going to tackle the interview. This makes things more unpredictable for the applicants; interviewers may follow a line of questioning quite inappropriate for the assessment they have to make, and that nobody would have thought likely to come up in that instance. However, even allowing for the whims of untrained interviewers, much can be done to anticipate what sort of things will be asked and to prepare accordingly. Certain topics are dealt with in just about all planned interviews and many of them come up in less well organised interviews too (though the latter often neglect to gather any information at all on some topics); so we shall now look at these most frequently encountered areas of questioning in some detail.

The Questions Asked, and Why

In this section, we shall look at eight main headings under which interviewers are likely to seek information, give some examples of the kind of questions asked and try to explain *why* they are asked. (A much fuller list of questions will be found in the Interview Preparation Programme and Checklist at the end of Chapter 5.) Different interviewers might categorise their topics to be covered in different ways from the one given here, but much the same information and kinds of questions would be involved.

The amount of time given to each of these areas in an interview, and the importance attached to the information obtained on any one topic, will vary according to individual circumstances. For example, for a school-leaver, the topic of work experience hardly arises, while education and training as an area of questioning will probably take a significant slice of the interview. The other point that should be noted here is that these eight topic areas inevitably overlap one another, and that the distinctions between them are slightly artificial. Interviewers may split up their task under these headings for convenience, but they will attempt to integrate all the information and use it to gain a picture of the 'whole' person.

Family background
The sort of questions might include:

'What is your father's job?' 'And your mother's?'
Have you any brothers or sisters? Are they older or younger than you?'
What work do they do?'
'What did your parents feel about you staying on at school to do "A" levels?'

Applicants are sometimes puzzled to encounter these questions, wondering what relevance they have to their own suitability for the job in question. There are a number of reasons for seeking this kind of information:

* An important one is to find out how well an individual has done in relation to the opportunities available to him or her. For example, a girl who gets a couple of 'A' levels with fairly modest grades and who does so against a background of financial hardship and lack of parental support or interest in her academic endeavours might well be adjudged to have achieved more than someone getting the same 'A' levels but coming from a comfortably-off family that also gave strong support and encouragement. This kind of assessment is clearly not an easy one to make, and the interviewers need to gather as much information as they can about the individual's family and their circumstances.

* With young job applicants, most of their lives so far have been spent in the context of the family and it can be expected to have exerted a vital formative influence on their personality and character (an influence that possibly does not decrease all that much even when they are older).

Family background and circumstances are two of the most important areas for an interviewer to cover if he is to get a full picture of the applicant, but ironically these matters are often missed out altogether or dealt with only very sketchily. The reason for this frequently turns out to be a reluctance on the part of interviewers to risk appearing intrusive. They often feel that asking questions in this area is a little like prying (which perhaps explains why questions like 'parents' occupation' are sometimes asked on the application form rather than in the interview). This is unfortunate, since few candidates object to these quite straightforward questions, even if they are not always quite sure of the point of them. Nor is there much reason for them to object, as the information obtained in this area very seldom actually produces evidence *against* a candidate but often puts him in a better light.

Education and training
Some of the questions here will simply be aimed at obtaining factual information or clearing up queries over exam results and grades, courses taken and so on. Most of the basic information will already be available to the interviewer if you have had to fill in an application form. The rest of the questions are a little different and probably require more thought, for example:

'Why did you choose to do economics at university rather than one of the subjects you took at advanced level in school?'
'What did you think were the best features of your degree course? What were the weakest aspects of it?'

'What subjects did you like most at school? What did you like least? Why?'

With young applicants who have either no work experience or only a minimal amount, the interview often centres strongly on the individual's education. *What* they have done is usually known. *Why* they did it, what they felt about it and the influence it has had on their attitudes and aspirations is the further information required. This has a bearing on motivation (see below) and can also reveal, in talking about likes and dislikes, what they did best and worst at school or college – something about their work aptitudes and preferences that may be relevant to the position the individual is applying for.

The non-academic aspects of school or college life may also be covered; things such as societies or clubs belonged to, positions of responsibility or authority held within the school or college and so on. The usefulness of this kind of questioning is that it can tell the interviewer something more about you as a person, your experience and your attitudes.

The questions encountered under this topic tend to be similar irrespective of the kind of institution involved, whether it be school, college or some other place of training.

Work experience

Once again, interviewers will probably have the main details of the person's work history outlined on the application form, and this will usually tell them where the individual worked, what the job title was and how long they were employed there. In order to assess the true relevance of this work experience to the post they are seeking to fill, interviewers need much more detail. So they should ask questions along the lines of those given below:

'You worked as an executive officer in the Department of Trade. What did this job involve?'
'What parts of the job did you like best? What parts did you like least?'

'What were the main problems you encountered in this work? How did you deal with them?'
'What were your colleagues like?'
'Why did you take the job in company X?'
'Why did you eventually leave company X?'

As will be gathered from this, interviewers have to find what duties were involved in the jobs the individual has done, and the implications that can be drawn about their ability to exercise responsibility, their supervising experience, the sort of training they have been given, and so on. This will help interviewers weigh up the extent to which individuals' previous jobs have contributed to their ability to do the one they are applying for now. Interviewers will also be interested in how they describe their colleagues and how they got on with them: are they likely to fit in here? The reasons given for taking and leaving jobs can also be very informative, often indicating what kinds of work applicants have not been happy with or suitable for in the past. If they have been through a whole string of jobs, none of them lasting very long, interviewers will very understandably want to know the reasons for such an unsettled work history.

With older applicants, previous work record is going to be perhaps the most significant part of the interview, because the type of work someone has done before, and how well they seem to have succeeded in various aspects of it, are going to be the most reliable indicators of how well they would be likely to make out in the post for which they are now being considered. Applicants with a considerable amount of work experience will not usually be questioned thoroughly on all of it, as interview time is very limited, so interviewers will often try to obtain their general views, preferences and attitudes regarding their previous employment and only go into detail on the most recent and/or most relevant jobs.

Although this area of questioning is not appropriate for school and college leavers, they may well have some vacation or other part-time work experience that attracts the interviewer's attention, in which case the kinds of question asked will probably be much the same as those given to someone in full-time employment. However, the scope and intensity of questioning is generally reduced if it is concerned only with vacation jobs, as is the usefulness of the answers in predicting how well the individual will cope with a permanent job.

Motivation and aspirations

It has been said that people can be divided into those who work to live and those who live to work. This is doubtless an over-simplification, but it does highlight the very real differences in the way people feel about their work and the kinds of satisfaction it provides for them. Interviewers may want to probe this area. They will want to assess your motivation towards work in general and, in particular, towards the kind of job they have to offer. This, however, is a rather difficult task because of the more abstract nature of the factors they are trying to assess. It is not the sort of area where they would be likely to say, 'Well, now I would like to discuss your motivation and aspirations'. Most interviewers would fight shy of such a bold approach to the subject, besides which there are very few questions that relate specifically to this part of an interview. More commonly, candidates' motivation and aspirations are inferred from what they have said in reply to other questions on other topics. In particular, the reasons they give for doing what they have done in the past (the decisions they have made in relation to education and work, and how those decisions were taken) may give some good pointers as to motivation and direction. There are some questions that can be put directly on this, for example:

'Why have you decided to apply for this job?'
'Where do you see yourself in, say, five years time?'
'What sort of work would you most like to do, given a free choice?'
'What would you do if you inherited a large sum of money?'

The reasons for asking the first question are pretty clear, though the value of the answer is not at all clear; many people (if they have any sense) have prepared an answer for that if for nothing else, and sometimes it is an answer framed more with what it is thought the interviewer would like to hear than with the truth in mind! We shall say more about this later.

The individual's aspirations are another concern. Do you have a clear, set (perhaps too set?) idea of what you want to do, or are you still making up your mind, or are you drifting along quite aimlessly? Are your ambitions realistic, too high or too low taking into account the scope of the job offered, the chances of progression in it and the evidence of your ability to date? Interviewers need to get answers to all of these questions, and mostly by gathering information indirectly. If they fail, they may find they have taken on someone who is going to be frustrated by the limitations of the post, or who will happily settle for a comfortable level of performance well below both what they are capable of and what is really needed. It can end up as an expensive and unfortunate mistake for either or both parties, you and the interviewer.

Leisure interests
Not always a feature of interviews, but quite common as a topic and one you should be prepared for. The range of questions is very large and will take any pastimes or leisure pursuits you have put down on the application form as the starting point. If no information on this has been asked for on the form or in any of the other papers then the interviewer will have to start from scratch:

'How do you spend your spare time?'
'Do you have any hobbies?'
'Do you play any sport?'
'I see you say reading is your main leisure activity. How many books do you get through each month? What do you get out of your reading? Have you a favourite author? Why do you like him in particular?'

The last series of questions is the sort of follow-up and probing interviewers have to do to establish whether the interest is a deep or even a genuine one. Apart from the depth of your interests, they may also try to assess the range of them. Why? Quite a few candidates are asked questions about what they do in their spare time and think to themselves, 'What on earth has this got to do with whether I am the right person for this job? What business is it of theirs anyway?' Well, there is some point in asking about leisure pursuits:

* It may say something about you as a person: do you, in general, go in for team or individual activities? Are your interests predominantly physical or intellectual? Do you take any part in organising leisure activities?

* If you are talking about something you are interested in and presumably know about, it should offer the interviewer an opportunity to assess how well you can express yourself. Do you explain things clearly? Do you convey your enthusiasm to others?

* The interests of an individual sometimes do (if he is particularly lucky) complement his work. And sometimes a keen interest in and obligations arising out of a pastime can be incompatible with the demands of a particular job (if it involves a great deal of travel, for example). So the interviewer will want to find out whether your interests (if any) are likely to supplement or supplant your contribution at work, or have no effect either way.

General topics

Again, this is optional in as much as it does not relate directly to your background, qualifications and so on. But some interviewers, mainly in the public service, ask questions on current affairs or social issues, such as:

'How do you think we should use the revenue we get from North Sea oil?'

'What are the arguments for and against the rapid development of nuclear power as an alternative energy source?'

Obviously, the questions will change according to the issues of the day, though they will generally steer clear of blatantly political or religious topics. If they do not, they are liable to find unsuccessful applicants attributing their failure to get the job to the notion that the interviewer's political or religious ideals differed from their own (which could indeed be the reason if the interviewer let the discussion on a topic degenerate into a heated political debate).

But why ask questions on topics like the Common Market, the education system or whatever?

* Interviewers want to see if you are aware of the world beyond your front gate and what is going on in it – in effect, to see if you take any interest in society as a whole.

* If you do (and you certainly *should*), interviewers may wish to find the extent to which you are able to form and express your opinions on topics. How articulate you are in presenting your case will be important in many areas of work.

* Allied to this is a wish to see if you are any good at defending your viewpoint on a topic. Interviewers will (if they are good) take on the role of devil's advocate and adopt a point of view opposite to your own simply to see how effectively you can support your idea in the face of opposition. Will you stick to your guns or will you collapse at the first sign of an argument? Have you 'thought through' your position on this topic? Do you know and understand the opposing viewpoint, or do you only look at things from one side of the fence?

All these questions and more may be in interviewers' minds when they discuss general topics with a candidate. Without any doubt, this can be one of the most stressful and testing parts of an interview, and one that really makes applicants 'think on their feet'. It is demanding for the interviewer too, and many of those who ask questions of this kind do not make a very good job of it – they simply get the candidate's views and neglect to challenge them in any way. Others quite unfairly expect the candidate to know about any subject they choose to light upon (all too often the interviewer's own pet interest). Some guidance on anticipating the kind of topics that are raised will be given in a later section (p. 61).

Specialist and technical matters
Clearly of importance in some jobs (mainly in scientific, technical or professional fields), some interviewers will concentrate quite heavily on testing specialist knowledge. A few go as far as to turn the interview into a kind of 'oral exam', but much more often this area of competence is assessed mainly on paper qualifications. However, there are a number of things that may induce an interviewer to test a candidate's specialist knowledge in the interview:

* The individual's paper qualifications may not be all that impressive and they may be a borderline case, so that any extra evidence on their technical expertise would be useful.

* More generally the motive might be to see how well applicants can explain aspects of their subject orally, and, in particular, whether they can convey technical concepts and procedures in a way that a non-specialist is able to understand.

* Interviewers could also ask questions of a sort that would seek to discover whether candidates had thought about the way in which their specialist knowledge related to the particular job applied for. This area is one more opportunity for the interviewer to get some idea of how quickly the candidate can think when placed under some pressure (as most candidates feel they are in the interview).

* One final reason for concentrating on technical topics in the interview is that these are the things the interviewer feels happiest talking about in some cases, as is often so with interviewers who are actually specialists in some area.

The range and type of questions on technical matters is vast and inevitably depends heavily on the field involved, so there is little point in trying to give specific examples here. The types of question that might come up (within the time limitations of an interview) will be apparent to the candidates in their respective fields, but note the advice given on p. 63. As a supplement to these questions, a candidate may be required to bring a workbook of projects or some other sample of work along to the interview to discuss.

Health

Very seldom do questions on the candidate's health come up. Other sources of evidence are used (either a note from the individual's physician, or a medical examination), or often nothing at all is asked on this. Application forms sometimes have questions relating to health and, if any incapacity or illness is declared on the form, applicants can expect that it will be followed up in the interview, should they get one. Some jobs clearly do require evidence of good health because of their physically demanding nature, but in these cases few interviewers would be sufficiently foolish to rest their assessment of applicants' health on their own subjective opinion on it.

Putting the Picture Together

Having asked questions in some or all of these areas, interviewers have to assemble their information and come to a conclusion. They have been building up a picture of the applicants from the first moment of the interview. This picture is not just a series of headings under which they have collected information; it should integrate the information in a way that will help the interviewers imagine what the applicants would actually be like doing the job. They will be asking themselves the sort of questions given below.

Does the applicant have a capacity for leading others?
Is he or she likely to be steady, and dependable?
Will he/she prove an acceptable colleague?
Has he/she sufficient (or even too much) self-confidence?

These are not things that can be asked directly in an interview, but will be inferred from answers given throughout the session.

The other important part of the overall impression created is whether the applicant has come over as a personable and pleasant individual; in other words, does he/she seem to have an agreeable disposition? This has been shown to be of primary importance to some interviewers, which is perhaps not too surprising (though still mistaken) if one assumes that *all* the candidates shortlisted for interviews are acceptable in terms of their basic qualifications anyway.

We have looked at the types of interview you are likely to encounter, at the approaches taken to them, and at the main areas under which interviewers seek information. In the following chapter we shall look at how this and other knowledge about interviews can be used in preparing for them. While doing this, it might be useful to keep in mind the reasons interviewers have for seeking the different kinds of information and to judge the sort of picture of you that they might build up from it.

5

Preparing for the Interview

Getting Practice

Practice helps performance in most things, and interviews are no exception. Practice can help interviewers *and* interviewees to improve their handling of the interview, particularly if it is practice under *guidance*. For the interviewers, this is no great problem because there are training courses they can attend where they will be given feedback on their performance as interviewers during practice sessions, usually supervised by psychologists. Such facilities are seldom available to job applicants, needless to say. There *are* some courses run at colleges that specifically aim to give feedback to candidates on their self-presentation in interviews but these are few and far between. If the chance arises to go on a course of this kind, by all means take it. Perhaps the next best thing is to volunteer to act as a 'guinea pig' candidate on courses for training interviewers; they have to interview someone in their practice sessions, and often seek volunteers to take the role of job applicants for this purpose. Not only do the volunteers generally get paid but the tutors on the course will be able and willing to counsel them on their interview performance. So again, if the opportunity should arise, by all means volunteer – it will probably prove an interesting, valuable and even financially rewarding experience!

These two limited chances of getting practice are the best, but by no means the only ones. It may be that career masters in schools or teaching staff in colleges can lay on some kind of practice sessions, with or without the aid of outside advisors (psychologists, personnel managers, etc.); if they do not do this at present and you would welcome such help, try asking to see if they have thought about arranging something of this kind. Practice without somebody being there to tell you the good and bad points of your 'performance' in the interview can also be useful, so you can get this practice by going for job interviews. Unfortunately, it is, of course, not very easy to get interviews and you cannot afford to treat them as just practice sessions when you do (unless it is a job you really do not want). Nevertheless, every interview provides some practice and if you review your own part in it as soon as possible afterwards, you can profit from the experience; this will be discussed in more detail on pp. 111–15.

Practice is of enormous help, and if you are lucky enough to find one of the courses referred to above, then all well and good. For the vast majority, however, the best (and indeed, only) help that is available may be the kind of written guidance provided here, allied to their own experience of actually being interviewed.

Finding Out About the Organisation

The organisations you apply to for jobs (in most cases) expect you to have some knowledge of the job in question and of the organisation itself. This is not unreasonable, since to select and train someone is normally an expensive process; if individuals drift into it without really knowing what to expect, they may very quickly find that it is not to their liking and leave, which is a waste of the organisation's time and money. So serious applicants will be expected to have taken the trouble to find out something about the job before applying for it. This would be the sensible thing to do anyway, but it is surprising how many applicants turn up for interviews with precious little idea of what the organisation or job is like.

You *should* already have a general impression of what the job involves and what the function of the employing organisation is when you make your initial application, but if you are given an interview it is worth doing a little more to further this knowledge. The sources of such information vary according to the job in question, but careers masters, college appointments boards, careers officers, friends and relatives may all be able to tell you something about the organisation and what it does. Quite possibly they will refer you to publications such as *The job book: training & career choices for school & college leavers* (Hobsons Press), which is readily available in libraries. On top of all this, many employers send out fairly detailed descriptions of both the job and the company as a whole with the application forms. Where they do this, careful reading of the material sent is frequently sufficient in itself.

If the organisation concerned is situated not very far from you, then perhaps you might kill two birds with one stone by going there to get any literature that may be available (such as the company's last annual report, which may also be obtained from the Company Secretary). Apart from the background information you may obtain, a visit to the place where the interview will be held will familiarise you with it and help you get the 'feel' of the place in advance, and may give you greater confidence.

You can also help yourself a lot by finding out about the selection procedures used by the different organisations. If you have an interview with the representatives of a company and know that one of your friends has already been seen by the same company, ask him or her about the interview, the kind of questions asked, whether or not any tests were given, and so on. Then you will know roughly what to expect. If you and your friend are in direct competition for the same job, you may of course meet with an unsympathetic response to your questions!

Reviewing and Preparing the Main Topic Areas

It is important to think about the interview in advance and to review the sort of information you may be asked for. From the last chapter you will have gathered that much of the interview is spent looking backwards at what you have done in the past, and why you have done it. If suddenly confronted with questions of this kind, the normal response of the applicant is to provide an answer as quickly as possible. Yet looking back over a period of some years may not be that easy and answers given on the spur of the moment in an interview may not be accurate; given time to think about questions of this sort, the applicant might give a very different answer (as some of them realise afterwards, prompting the reaction, 'Why on earth did I say that?'). It is best to think over these sort of questions in advance as far as possible. And it *is* possible: with a degree of intelligent anticipation, you can spot the sort of questions that are likely to arise. Some clue is often given by the application form; if it asks for information about family background (e.g. parents' occupations) then this may be seen as being of some relevance and will quite possibly be followed up with questions in the interview. Likewise, if the form asks you to list interests, the interviewer will probably pick up on this and ask questions about those leisure pursuits you have listed. It was suggested in Chapter 2 that you should photocopy the application form after completing it; if you did this, you should refer to the form prior to the interview. Apart from the clues you might get from the application form, and anything you hear from other people you know who have been interviewed by the same organisation, the guidance given here should (with a little intelligent application on your part) also assist in forming some expectations of the type of things you are likely to be asked.

In order to structure your preparation and thinking about interviews, an Interview Preparation Programme and Checklist is provided at the end of this chapter (pp. 72–8). This shows, in detail, the sort of questions interviewers ask and covers most of the topics that they are likely to introduce. If you now turn to it briefly you will see how it is laid out and what it consists of. This structured guide to self-review should be gone through slowly, as the instructions tell you, after you have read the rest of this book. For the moment, all we need to do here is make some general points about preparing for questions under each of the main topic areas discussed previously. The emphasis should be on identifying the sort of information *you* wish to get across in the interview as well as coping adequately with the interviewer's questions.

_____

Family background

These questions are fairly straightforward, predictable and easy to answer. Sometimes applicants are reluctant to let an interviewer know that they have come from a relatively disadvantaged background, but as was pointed out on p. 42 this information can work to their credit if the interviewer is trying to assess how well they have done in light of the opportunities open to them. So do *not* be shy about putting across facts that are going to work in your favour; if you had a steep hill to climb to get where you are now, let it be known. Your circumstances in the past often lead on to consideration of your circumstances at present. This is where female applicants face the potentially hazardous questions of marital and family aspirations. Interviewers may justify asking questions about whether a woman is married and whether she intends having children as simply trying to get a fuller picture of her as a person. But, notwithstanding equal opportunities legislation, one suspects some of them will treat the information that a woman intends giving up work (even temporarily) to have a family as being a reason for not employing them. In a situation of this kind, perhaps the applicant is within her rights if she says something along the lines of 'I really have not thought seriously about that [having children] yet, so I could not say', or 'I am not sure whether I will or not', or just 'No, I do not want to have any children – at least, that's the way I feel about it now.' When thinking about this, it is worth remembering that the use of such information in making selection decisions is a breach of the law in most cases anyway.

Education and training

Again, these questions are, on the whole, easy to cope with providing you have given them a little thought beforehand. A poor record in examinations can be a little tricky if it is mentioned. Interviewers sometimes ask if there is any special reason for doing badly in some or all of the examinations; if there is, by all means give it. Unfortunately, if you make too much of it, there is a danger that it will be dismissed as 'just making excuses'. So do not play too heavily on your excuses, no matter how genuine they are; it might be better, for example, to mention the extenuating circumstances but admit that you do not know just how much difference they have made to the final results (though the implication may be 'a lot').

Generally, an ability to form and express opinions on your education and training is one of the things the interviewer will look for. The important thing to note is that an endless recital of criticisms is in itself unlikely to win you any applause; you should try to be constructive in your views. So if you have a criticism of the way a course is run or of the type of institution you are attending, be prepared not only to make that point but also to suggest how you feel things could be improved.

Work experience

If you have any work experience, the aspects of it to think about in advance of the interview are:

* The reasons you had for joining and leaving the organisations you have worked for,

* what you did in those jobs which you can point to as relevant and useful to the job you are applying for now,

* what you were especially successful at,

* how you dealt with the problems,

* how you got on with colleagues.

All these entail refreshing your memory and thinking over, otherwise your answers may seem vague and hesitant and generally lacking in conviction. If you seem uncertain and vague about the reasons for taking and leaving the jobs you have had, the impression will be that you have drifted aimlessly through them. Particular care must be taken in considering what you will say (and how it will be interpreted) concerning your reasons for wanting to leave your present job and join *this* organisation.

Motivation and aspirations

There are very few direct questions on this. As we saw earlier, most of what the interviewer knows of the candidate's motivation and aspirations is inferred from what the candidate says over the course of the interview. If you do have an idea of what you want to do now and in the near future, you will come across as being a person who knows where they are going, which will probably be to the good. The value of knowing something about the job and the company comes when the interviewer asks why you want this job and what specifically attracts you to it; your level of motivation will not impress if you have not got the faintest idea of what it is all about. However, there is no need to imply that this is absolutely the only kind of job you have considered.

Looking further ahead in time, the interviewer might ask 'How do you see your career developing over, say, the next five years?' It is as well to have given some thought to how you would like things to go, providing this is coloured by reality – but obviously any such aspirations should not be inflexible. People and circumstances change over time, so any ideas you have now on how you want your career to develop should not be too fixed. The interviewer is unlikely to be much more impressed by someone with a very rigid set of aims for the future than by someone who as yet has no aims at all. Another aspect of this is the degree of ambition you show. A dim view is likely to be taken of anyone who is devoid of ambition, but the same sometimes goes for a candidate who has a very high level of ambition; the excessively ambitious may be hard to satisfy and leave the company after a year or two, before the investment in them in the form of recruitment and training provides any return.

One type of question that does not fit well under any of the normal headings, but which might be loosely related to motivation, is the one that invites you to assess your own strengths and weaknesses (in general and in relation to the job) in a very direct fashion. In other words, questions that require you to 'sell' yourself. Sometimes they are delivered with all the subtlety of a sledge-hammer – 'What makes you think you would do this job well?' A more lethal form of this can come before the interview, when a candidate may be asked to write a description of himself, first as if written by a friend and then as if written by a critic. We will have more to say on the handling of questions like this later, but for the moment you should think about them for yourself.

* What experience, training, qualifications and personal qualities are there in your favour relevant to the job?

* What are your strengths overall?

* What weaknesses are there in your abilities, experience, etc., and what would the interviewer's reaction be to them?

If you did not admit to any weaknesses, e.g. being bad at figure-work, would you be believed? Would you believe anyone who said that? Questions of this kind are difficult and need a lot of thought in advance.

Finally, one direct question that often comes up and may be taken as an indication of your motivation is

'Are you willing to move to another part of the
country if the company wants you to?'

Mobility may be a vital requirement of the job, so you
had better decide beforehand whether you are willing
to be moved around the country. Do not dismiss
the idea too quickly, as moving around can help you
develop as an individual, quite apart from increasing
your employment prospects.

Leisure interests
These should be fairly easy for you to talk about. One of
the main dangers is 'freezing' in the interview when
asked things like 'I see you like reading. What was the
last book you read?' Normally such questions would be
simple, but many an interviewee will testify to the
wonderful ease with which the mind goes blank at
moments like this, with the result that the interviewer
begins to doubt whether you really do any reading at
all. A little thought in advance about the likely questions should reduce the chances of this kind of mental
paralysis gripping you.
    Two points that frequently arise are:

* Just how much time do you have to spend on a pursuit
  for it to be an interest? There is no simple answer
  to this; it remains a matter of judgement. Resist the
  temptation to give almost everything you ever do as an
  interest. For instance, if you claim that you are interested
  in the theatre and it is discovered that you have been
  only once in the last year, you are going to look a trifle
  foolish (barring extenuating circumstances, such as
  long distance, finance, etc.). If you are going to give a
  particular activity as one of your leisure pursuits it
  should be something that you do fairly regularly and
  which you feel you can talk about if asked. You should
  go for depth of interest rather than a large range of
  shallow interests.

* Should one mention only interests that are likely to
  impress interviewers? By all means emphasise the more

socially impressive interests to an interviewer if you have a range of things to which you devote more or less equal amounts of time. But do not try to paint a false picture of your leisure activities in the hope of making yourself look good. If you depart far from the truth in this respect, the interviewers are quite likely to find you out, which may discredit you in every other way too.

Another aspect of this is that some candidates feel that the things they do in their time off are somehow not 'respectable' enough to give as interests. These include activities such as watching television, listening to rock and roll music and going out with friends to parties, pubs, etc. In fact, most interviewers would be surprised if candidates (particularly young ones) did not spend some of their time doing these things. They may not be 'formal' interests such as chess, football, photography, literature and so on, but they are certainly better to mention than nothing at all. And if you do have *no* interests at all due to some particular personal circumstances, make sure the interviewer realises that there are reasons for this lack of activity.

Remember!
If there are any indications that you are particularly good at one of your hobbies (e.g. representing your college in it), or if you take some part, no matter how modest, in organising leisure activities for others (secretary of a society, for instance), try to ensure that this information is conveyed in the interview if the chance arises: make it one of your objectives to get this across in the interview.

General topics
There are four main sources of these topics:

* things in the news at the time,

* things related to the job or the organisation,

* things the applicant says in the course of the interview or on the application form, and

* (worst of all) anything that happens to interest the interviewer.

How can you prepare for these? Well there is not a great deal you *can* do, which is precisely the point (or one of them) of asking questions on current affairs, social issues and so forth – you have to 'think on your feet' in dealing with the questions. One useful step is to read the newspapers and watch news and current affairs programmes on TV thoroughly during the period you are applying for jobs (even if you do not do so normally); then you will at least be familiar with what is going on and can spot anything that looks particularly relevant to this job or to this organisation and its operations. If you have also formed views of your own on the main issues, all the better. Remember here that the interviewers are unlikely to ask questions on overtly political or religious matters, so that cuts down the field somewhat. However, the range of possible topics is still formidable. Fortunately, there is a tendency to concentrate on the 'big' issues – just one example would be energy policy and the pros and cons of investing in a large-scale nuclear power programme; try thinking of some others yourself.

As far as topics arising out of your comments or application form are concerned, these will probably relate to things that you know something about and have views on anyway. Wider issues relating to the organisation's functions or products are topics that can be anticipated to some extent.

The real problem comes from the interviewer's own particular interests. It is quite unfair for interviewers to expect candidates to be able to talk about anything they choose to light upon, but they sometimes seem to expect precisely that. If this happens, you can try to bluff your way through or admit that this just happens to be a topic you know little or nothing about; the latter course is the better bet.

Specialist and technical matters

Potentially, anything relating to your specialist field could be asked. Fortunately, however, some narrowing down of this wide range can again be achieved by prior consideration. Questions in this area are most often focused on any project work the candidate has done (or on any other indication of their specialised interest within their discipline), or on the application of their training to particular facets of the job they are applying for. In thinking over these themes when preparing for an interview, it is as well to keep in mind that the interviewers are not always specialists, or specialists of the same kind as the candidate – in effect, they are laymen. It is thus wise to think in terms of having to communicate technical information in a way that anyone can understand. Some specialists who carry out interviews do ask questions of a technical nature over a wide area of the subject concerned. Clearly, you cannot revise everything just for an interview, but it might be wise to brush-up on your weakest points.

Health

No preparation needed. If you have indicated some physical handicap or history of illness on the application form and this is taken up in the interview, you will no doubt be all too well aware of it to need any consideration beforehand.

The Unpredictable Elements

In case you have now slipped into the cosy notion that interviews, given sensible preparation, are entirely predictable, it is important that you be dragged back to reality. *No* interview is 100% predictable or anything like it. There are always surprises, things you did not expect, even if it follows the kind of planned approach in exactly the same way as described here. This should not frighten you though (after all, what worthwhile and interesting conversation ever runs *exactly* according to expectations – if it did, it would be rather dull). Looking at an interview in a positive light, as a potentially interesting and stimulating experience, you should welcome a reasonable degree of unpredictability as a challenge. What one wants to avoid is an interview in which, through the interviewees being quite unprepared, *every question* comes as something unexpected. The result of the latter is that interviewees may never really get comfortable in responding to the straightforward questions, let alone achieving the state of mind where they are ready to respond to the more challenging ones.

Rehearsal: the Best Laid Plans . . .

Another warning note should be sounded here. All the guidance given on preparing for interviews, including the Interview Preparation Programme and Checklist, is intended to direct your memory and thought to the areas and types of questioning you are most likely to encounter; they are *not* there to help you to form precise answers that can be recited in the interview.

Rehearsing word-perfect answers is not a good idea at all. We have just talked about the unpredictable elements of interviews, and one aspect of this is that questions you may be expecting seldom come out in *precisely* the way you anticipated. You might, for example, be expecting the question 'What are your leisure interests?', but the actual question asked is 'What do you get out of your leisure interests?' Hearing the word 'leisure interests' will trigger off your carefully prepared response, which may well neglect the real nature of the question. So, in this example, you might start by replying along the lines of 'Well, I play a lot of sport; I enjoy football particularly, and I suppose I do quite a lot of reading . . .' This is not a reply to the question asked, it is a reply to the question anticipated. If you persist in doing this (not quite answering the question as posed) the interviewer may well become somewhat irritated, or may conclude that, for some reason best known to youself, you are being deliberately evasive.

Apart from this tendency to give prepared answers irrespective of the wording of the question, there is the other danger that precisely formulated answers have a nasty habit of not coming out quite as they were meant to in the interview.

Perhaps the only time one would be advised to think out the wording of a reply in detail beforehand would be where specialist or technical questions are likely to be asked. For example, if you have done a thesis or project, you will very often be asked about it. The interviewer, if he is a specialist in the same general areas as you, may still not be all that familiar with this particular topic, so if you are describing the project work to him it is important that you can put it across clearly and concisely. If you have reason to believe that the interviewers (or some of them) may be non-specialists or administrators, then it is even more important that you can convey what you have done in a non-technical way. To do this, and to do it in such a way that it can be communicated in a very limited amount of time, requires considerable thought in advance of the interview. In this instance, some actual rehearsal of a pre-planned answer may well pay dividends.

Preparing Your Own Questions

Questioning in interviews is seldom an entirely one-way process. You will usually be given a chance to put questions of your own at the end of the interview. This is not meant for you to ask, as I heard one applicant ask, 'Where can I get a No. 37 bus?' It is your opportunity to fill in the gaps in your information about the job, working conditions, promotion prospects, etc. Quite apart from the value of finding answers to your questions, it is probably in your interests to have some questions to ask, if only for the sake of appearances. Interviewers will be more inclined to judge a candidate's intentions as being 'serious' if they show a lively interest in the job and future prospects. Again, the best strategy is to get clear in your mind the questions you want to ask before you go to the interview, otherwise you are likely to find, as many have before you, that at the end of an (often searching) interview you are mentally fatigued and your mind goes blank when you are offered the chance to ask questions.

Incidentally, do not make the questions too numerous or too detailed; the interviewer, in large organisations anyway, cannot know all the details of all the jobs that may eventually be open to you. Also, he has limited time, so you must gauge the extent to which he is willing to go on answering questions.

Adopting the Right Attitude

If you do not get very worked up over attending interviews, then you have little problem in this respect. You can of course be over-confident and not take things as seriously as they should be. I remember having an interview for a job that I was not sure whether or not I wanted. I found myself getting quite tense waiting outside the interview room and so I thought 'This is ridiculous – getting worked up over a job that I'm not sure I want.' I started thinking about the negative aspects of the job, and when I was called in a few minutes later, I had thought myself into the mood where I did not care very much whether the job was offered or not. This relatively detached attitude was of itself no bad thing, but no sooner had the four-man selection board introduced themselves in a very business-like and efficient manner than there was a loud 'thud'. All eyes turned toward the windows from whence this noise came, and outside we saw the top of a ladder, from which rapidly sprouted a window-cleaner clutching a bucket and sponge. He proceeded to noisily clean the windows while the interview was in progress. The consternation and embarrassment this caused the board, along with the sheer silliness of the situation which appealed to my sense of humour, combined to make me wildly over-confident. I found it difficult to take the proceedings seriously and started cracking jokes. Needless to say, I did not get the job! I ascertained afterwards that my attitude in the interview was the main thing that went against me.

I mention this anecdote simply to show that one can be *too* relaxed and confident in an interview. To be just a little anxious, a little keyed-up about interviews is good: it generally facilitates performance rather than inhibits it. Only when you become very anxious do you begin to harm your prospects. Some advice on how to 'keep your cool' in this kind of situation will be given in later sections of this chapter and the next, but, if you tend to get over-anxious about interviews, your first concern should be your overall attitude towards them. One of the problems here is that some candidates see interviews as basically threatening situations: they worry about their own deficiencies, about how nervous they get, about what the interviewers will think of them, about failing to get the job, and so on. It is as if the 'fear of failure' overcomes their 'need for achievement'. Stressing the negative aspects of the procedure like this does little good. If you can, try to reconstrue the interview in a more positive light. This, admittedly, is easy to say but not so easy to do. However, the following lines of thought have proved helpful to others and may also be useful to you in this respect.

---

* If you can arouse some curiosity in the procedure it can help make it a more pleasant experience. What sort of things will they ask, what sort of approach will they take, what sort of person are they after? Treat it like a guessing game, a battle of wits: can you anticipate the interviewers and prepare accordingly? This outlook makes the interview more of an interesting and challenging experience. And the more interested you are, the more that interest will convey itself in the interview itself, which will do you no harm at all.

---

* Alternatively, you may prefer to look on the interview as a joint problem-solving exercise between you and the interviewer in which you will cooperate together to find whether this is really the job for you, whether you would be able to do it well, and whether you would be happy doing it.

---

* Another strategy is to go in to the interview with low expectations, saying to yourself 'I probably have not got a chance of this job, but I will do as well as I can in

the interview because it will be good practice for other occasions'. Mentally writing off your chances in this way obviously has its dangers (as has the similar approach of trying to persuade yourself that this job probably is not all that good anyway), but it can create a more relaxed and detached approach that can be helpful to some people.

* Others may be happier if they can look on the bright side and keep in mind that, of all the people to apply for this job, they are amongst the very few selected for interview, so they must be suitable on paper at very least.

These different ways of thinking about the interview all have their advantages and disadvantages. Whether or no you use any of them is for you to decide; choose whichever you feel most comfortable with and easiest to sustain.

Personal Appearance and Dress

While there is no doubt that views on what is and what is not acceptable in terms of personal appearance and dress have relaxed considerably over recent years, you should not be lulled into thinking that this is no longer important. Most interviewers are willing to accept (in some cases perhaps it is more a case of 'resigned to') candidates with long hair, flamboyant styles and colours of clothing and so on, *providing* they are neat, clean and smart in appearance. So, while it is not necessary (unless you want to play really safe) to have a short back and sides haircut and to don the most conservative suit you can lay hands on, it is wise to take some care over your appearance and to turn up in something a bit more impressive than denim.

For candidates of either sex, it is important that they show they have taken some care over their appearance for the interview; after all, if they cannot be bothered about how they look on this occasion, the interviewer will have just cause for doubting whether they will when they are working either, which may be important in some jobs where the individual will be representing the organisation. The other thing here, of course, is that an interviewer may, rightly or wrongly, infer something about how serious a candidate's interest in a job is from how much attention he or she has paid to personal appearance.

So remember!
Make sure that your hair, finger nails, shoes and clothes are all clean; it is surprising how many people neglect one or other of these.

One sometimes hears the view expressed that applicants should dress as they like and not put on any special effort for the benefit of an interview, because if it is the kind of organisation that cares so much about such superficial things as how someone looks then it probably is not worth working for anyway. Applicants who say this are in effect selecting themselves *out* of companies whose values they think they probably do not share. Well, fine – that is their right if they so wish. One of the problems with this strategy, however, is that interviewers are not always truly representative of the climate and values of the organisations they are recruiting for. So a candidate may be rejected because of his appearance simply on the basis of the interviewer's prejudices, while if he had been taken in to that organisation he might have found a far more relaxed and congenial atmosphere that suited him perfectly.

It is certainly true that one can no more tell which is the best candidate by his or her appearance than one can judge a book by its cover. Judging by appearances is apt to be misleading. None the less, first impressions are very powerful, and the interviewer's first impressions of an applicant are strongly coloured by the personal appearance of the latter. And in some cases there *is* good reason for assessing people on their appearance, as in the case of jobs where the individual will have a high degree of public contact, and should thus be very 'presentable'. Even if the job in question is not of this kind, there is often the possibility that later transfers or promotions will put an individual in a position that does have representative duties.

Finally, apart from dressing in clothes that will look good, try to make sure that you *feel* good in them too. Avoid things which are too heavy or thick, or too tight or anything else that is likely to make you feel uncomfortable (e.g. some people find nylon shirts tend to make them perspire when they are tense) in the interview. Ideally, you want to dress in clothes that are not only neat and smart, but in which you feel *relaxed* and comfortable as well.

Immediately before the Interview

There are a few sensible steps you can take just before the interview which can help you, not least in respect of your state of mind when you arrive.

Travelling

It may sound like a statement of the obvious, but you need to work out precisely where you are going, and how to get there, well in advance. A surprising number of candidates manage to turn up late because they have not done this. You must leave yourself an adequate safety margin in timing your journey to take account of the vagaries of public transport, traffic jams, etc. Delays on the journey, even if they do not actually make you late, can cause anxiety if you have not left yourself adequate time. You can do without worries of this kind, so do not cut things too fine. A more leisurely paced journey will leave you in a better mental state.

Relaxation

Comments relating to this have already been made in connection with the clothes you wear, your travel arrangements and your general attitude. There is no one single trick that will ensure a relaxed feeling in the interview. There are special deep relaxation techniques but these are time-consuming and need expert supervision.

If you are the sort of individual who gets very nervous waiting for an interview, you might try the following technique: close your eyes, breathe in and out *evenly*, *slowly* and *deeply* and say (to yourself) 'One' each time you breathe out. Concentrate on your breathing, and gradually relax your body as much as possible; focus your attention on different groups of muscles in succession (e.g. back of the neck and shoulders, stomach, legs) until you are as relaxed as you can get. This kind of relaxation technique used before an interview sometimes helps produce a more calm yet alert state of mind, particularly if it has been practised on a number of occasions.

One type of relaxing agent *not* recommended is alcohol. It may make you feel better to have a couple of drinks before an interview, but the anaesthetic effect will probably impair your concentration, and anyway interviewers are not notorious for the generosity of their assessments when they detect the smell of beer or spirits wafting across from the candidate (sucking mints is a woefully inadequate remedy).

You can help yourself a great deal, not just in relaxing but in terms of your whole state of mind, by ensuring you get a good night's sleep the night before the interview. So try to arrange things in such a way that you avoid anything that will keep you up very late and leave you feeling tired and left-over the next day.

And talking of basic needs or functions do not forget the wonderfully laxative quality interviews sometimes have! Go to the toilet before you set out on your journey, and leave yourself enough time to go again (if needs be) before entering the interview room.

One other point about keeping calm before the interview. Should you have left a safety margin in the timing of your journey and arrived a little early, you can kill time by having a look around the area or by simply sitting in the waiting room. Either way, it is often a good idea to take something to read – the more engrossing the better!

Interview Preparation Programme and Checklist
This programme pulls together the main points of the advice given in this chapter. If you follow it carefully, you will be about as well prepared as anyone can be to face the interview.

Stage I: General Preparation

☞ Obtain details and background information about the organisation concerned. Find out anything you can about its method of selecting people, and about the kinds of questions asked in the interview.

☞ Visit the place where the interviews will be held if this is not too far away. Apart from getting the feel of the place and collecting any background literature, you can check the transport arrangements when doing this dry-run.

☞ Be sure you know how to get to the interview location (ideally by the method outlined above). Look at the relevant timetables for transport and arrange things so that you have an adequate margin if any delays occur.

☞ Remember to present as neat, clean and tidy an appearance as possible (wash your hair, get your clothes cleaned, etc.).

☞ Re-read the copy of the application form if you have kept one. Take the letter giving the time and date of the interview with you.

☞ Work through the questions listed below.

Stage II: Question Preparation
The questions listed below are frequently asked in interviews, though not always in quite the form given here. For the purposes of the present exercise, some questions that are related and would come in a sequence during an interview have been run together. Also you

should note that whether a question is put in the past tense or present tense is irrelevant; simply take it as being in the tense that applies to you (e.g. when a question about your college course is worded as if you have left when in fact you are still at college). The actual wording of the questions in the interview may be different from that given here, but the information and thought required from you will be much the same.

The questions have been put under a few headings representing the main topic areas. Inevitably, some of this categorising is arbitrary and some of the questions could come under any of several headings as they provide information about them. Work through the questions slowly. Not all of them will apply to everyone, of course, so use your own sense in identifying those not relevant to you. Some very basic, mundane questions have been included and these will take very little time to deal with. The trickier questions deserve more time and consideration. With each one you should first think about the information asked for and then consider how to put it across, with the accent on a positive approach. Consider how your answers might be received by other people.

FAMILY BACKGROUND

- What does your father do for a living?

- Does your mother work? If so, what does she do?

- Have you any brothers and sisters? Older or younger than you? Do they work, and if so, what do they do?

- What is/was life like at home?

- Did you spend your childhood in one area, or did you move around a lot?

- If you did move around, what effect (if any) did this have on you?

- How did your parents feel about (a) you staying on/ leaving school, (b) going to college, (c) applying for this kind of job?

- What influence have your parents had on the decisions you have taken in your life?

- If you no longer live at home now, how did you feel about leaving home?

- Are you thinking of getting married in the near future?

EDUCATION AND TRAINING

The first five groups of questions apply to both school and college or university:

- What did you think of it? What did you like best about the place, and what least? Why?

- What subjects (or parts of them) were you best at, and why? Which subjects were you least good at, and why?

- What subjects did you like best? Why? Which subjects did you like least? Why?

- What guided your choice of subjects/courses?

- Do your examinations results fairly reflect your ability? If not, give your reasons for believing they do not.

- Why did you stay on at school (or, why did you not stay on)?

- Why did you/did you not choose to go to college?

- Did you consider any alternatives to continuing your education? Why did you reject them?

- Why did you go to that particular college?

- What do you think of the course? How could it be improved?

- What do you think of this country's system of higher education? Would you make any changes in it – if so, what and why?

- Did you do any special projects at college? Describe them, briefly.

- Have you done any postgraduate or any other research work? If so, describe it in terms that a non-specialist could understand.

- *(In relation to any college projects or postgraduate work.)* What implications do the results have? What applications does the work have? What relevance does it have for job and the kind of work it involves?

- What did you get out of your time at college?

- Do you pursue any educational courses in your own time?

- Do you speak any foreign languages? How well?

WORK EXPERIENCE
In regard to any full-time job, and also some part-time jobs, the following questions can come up:

- How/why did you come to take this job?

- What did your particular job entail – what did you actually have to do?

- What skills/qualities were needed?

- What did you like and dislike about it? Why?

- Were you good at it? If not, why?

- How would you have improved the job, given the chance?

- Were you promoted, or have any other increase in your responsibilities, while you were in the job?

- What was the most difficult aspect of it?

- What problems did you encounter? How did you tackle them?

- How did you get on with your colleagues?

- What did you get out of the job? What did you learn from it? How does it relate to the job that you are applying for now – what help would it be to you?

- Why did you leave? Why do you want to leave?

- Have you any experience of managing staff? If so, give details. If not, how do you feel you would cope with it?

- Have you done any figure work (accounts, etc.) in your jobs? Do you like that sort of work? How good are you with figures?

- Do you know much about computers? Have you any experience of working with them?

MOTIVATIONS AND ASPIRATIONS

- What do you know about this organisation, and about its products or services?

- Who is the head man or woman in it?

- Has this organisation been in the news at all recently?

- Have any developments (social, economic, political, scientific or technological) of the recent past got any particular implications for this organisation and its products or services? If so, what are they?

- Why do you want this job? What appeals to you about it?

- Has anyone given you any advice that helped persuade you to apply for this? Who?

- What alternatives to this job are you considering, if any?

- If you have considered and rejected them, why?

- Which part of the organisation's function are you most interested in? Why?

- Are you willing to move to another part of the country if the firm needs to send you there?

- Would you want a job that involves a lot of travelling round?

- How would you feel about working irregular hours or overtime if required?

- Why do you think you will be good at this job? What evidence can you point to in support of this?

- What are your strengths and weaknesses?

- What do you want out of a job?

- How do you see your career developing over the next few years?

- What do you think you will do if you do not get this particular job?

LEISURE INTERESTS

- What do you do in your spare time?

- Which of your leisure interests is the main one?

- How much time to you devote to activity X? How good are you at it? What pleasure or satisfaction do you get from it? How long have you been doing it?

- Have you ever achieved any particular success in one of your leisure pursuits?

- Have your spare-time activities ever involved you in an organising role?

(The following questions could apply equally to films, the theatre or other arts-oriented interests)

- Do you like reading? How many books a month/year do you get through?

- What is your favourite type of reading?

- What was the last book you read?

- Who is your favourite writer? Why?

GENERAL TOPICS; SPECIALIST AND TECHNICAL MATTERS
By their nature, these will vary so much from individual to individual and from interview to interview that the same kind of question preparation is not possible; simply follow the general advice given earlier in this chapter (pp. 61–3). One set of questions that does often come up, however, is:

- Do you read a newspaper? Which one? Why? Which section of the paper do you turn to first?

In terms of specialist fields, a device sometimes used by interviewers for sales jobs is to point to a pen or ash tray on the table and say to the candidate – 'Right, persuade me that I want to buy this.'

6

Putting Yourself Across in the Interview

Testing Your Own Ideas as a Starting Point
How should you act in the interview? Everyone seems to have their own idea. Some people see it as a joint problem-solving exercise between the job applicant and the interviewer to find out whether this person and this job are right for one another. At the other extreme, some interviewees see it as a battle of wits, the interviewers doing their damnedest to discover some reason why you should not get this job while you do your utmost to foil them. In between these two ends of the spectrum, all sorts of questions rise – like, is it wise to argue with an interviewer? should I try to bluff my way through if I don't know the answer? is it best to try to hide your weakest areas? There are, of course, numerous other books and pamphlets on how to deal with interviews, but the majority of them rest on the experience and views of one, or maybe two people, namely the authors. You would get a much better idea of what is expected of you in the interview if you could get the opinions of a large group of personnel officers and other recruitment interviewers. And this is exactly what you will have here. I asked over 120 people in the personnel field who are heavily involved in selection

interviewing what advice they would give on how to deal with the interview, and their replies are represented in this chapter.

Before consuming all this wisdom, however, you might like to do a short quiz (see facing page) to test out some of your present ideas on how to behave in interviews. When you have completed it, carry on and read through the chapter; we will come back to the quiz and your answers at the end.

Reception, and the Importance of First Impressions
We saw earlier (p. 28) that interviewers sometimes make up their minds about candidates too early on in the interview, and we know from our everyday lives that first impressions can have a powerful and long-lasting effect. When we have a set or expectancy to see people a particular way, we go on seeing them that way because we tend to ignore information that contradicts our viewpoint or we interpret the new information so that it is made to fit in with our existing perceptions. The early part of the interview is thus very important, all the more so with interviews being so short anyway – if you get off on the wrong foot there is not a lot of time to put things right. Fortunately, some interviewers make allowances for nerves, etc. at the start of an interview, but you cannot count on that. So let us look at how you tackle the introduction.

Introductions

* First things first: when you enter the interview room, do not forget to close the door behind you.

* As you face the interviewer(s), try to raise a quiet smile and walk over to the chair ready for you, but do not sit down until invited to do so.

* The way interviewers greet you varies enormously; they are often not sure themselves how best to do it so that it puts you at ease. Some go the whole hog and

Look at the rating scales below; each one describes an aspect of how to behave in an interview and gives a pair of alternative strategies. Decide which of each pair offers the best advice on how to tackle an interview and tick that side of the rating scale (the more strongly you feel that to be the best way of behaving, the closer to that end of the scale you should tick).

1 Be assertive |—1—2—3—4—5—| Be submissive

2 Look serious |—1—2—3—4—5—| Smile a lot

3 Keep a lot of eye contact with the interviewer |—1—2—3—4—5—| Avoid much eye contact with the interviewer

4 Do not hesitate before giving your answers |—1—2—3—4—5—| Take your time in answering questions

5 Be willing to argue a point with the interviewer |—1—2—3—4—5—| Go along with the interviewer and do not disagree

6 Say as much as possible |—1—2—3—4—5—| Say as little as possible

7 When you do not know the answer admit it |—1—2—3—4—5—| When you do not know an answer try to bluff your way through

8 Do not let silences develop – keep on talking |—1—2—3—4—5—| Do not respond to silences

9 Say nothing about your weaker points unless forced to |—1—2—3—4—5—| Be open about your limitations

10 Sell yourself – tell them why you should get the job |—1—2—3—4—5—| Play it straight

stand up, shake you by the hand and introduce themselves and (if it is a board interview) their colleagues.
Others simply stay seated and issue a perfunctory
greeting. You just have to play this as it comes, but do
not offer to shake hands unless the interviewer proffers
his.

* If it is difficult for you to remember names first time
round – and in board interviews it is even more difficult – make a conscious effort to do so at this point; it
helps if you can quickly use the name after you are
introduced by saying 'Good morning Mr Smith' or
'How do you do, Mrs Davies', or whatever.

* Irrespective of the kind of greeting you get, *look the
interviewer in the eye*. Likewise with board interviews,
do not just look at the Chairperson, give the others a
brief glance and smile too (maybe even a nod!). You do
not have to keep this smile plastered grimly to your
face; it is really only a good thing to do when you come
in, are introduced, at appropriate lighter moments in
the interview and when you say goodbye.

To sum up the introduction. Take your lead from the
interviewer, look at him, put on a reasonably pleasant
face and try to appear as if you are glad to be there even
if you feel as though you are facing a firing squad.

Combating Interview Nerves

This was looked at in terms of preparation in the
previous chapter. The better your preparation, the more
confident you are likely to be. However, all but a few
people will still feel a little tense in interviews. In fact, if
it is any compensation, even some of the interviewers
do too. What can you do to keep calm when you are
actually in there?

* Try to sit comfortably without actually slouching.

* Do *not* smoke unless you are invited to do so (if you

desperately need a cigarette, you might risk asking if it is all right).

* Do not chew gum or anything else either, as I have seen one or two people do!

* Take your time over your answers to questions; a common mistake is to blurt out the first thing that comes into one's head, which soon makes things seem worse. Give yourself a second or two before answering, and consciously check yourself if you are talking much faster than normal. You can, of course, be too slow and deliberate in answering, but few people go this far and rushing your answers is a much greater danger.

* Sometimes an interviewer or members of a panel may, perhaps because of their manner or because someone is silly enough to try deliberately to put stress on you, seem rather threatening and hostile; obviously, this is very off-putting. If you encounter this kind of situation and experience a lot of anxiety, you might find a technique used by allied prisoners-of-war of some value. If a guard was being particularly threatening – say, shouting angrily in the prisoner's face – the POW would try to imagine him exactly as he was, standing there in front of him and shouting his head off, but stark naked. It is wonderful how much dignity and authority depart with one's clothing. Providing you have just a little imagination, this technique can work extremely well with bombastic or arrogant interviewers too. All you have to do is to imagine them, sitting there behind their desk with all their papers in front of them – but stark naked! If your imagination is vivid, I should warn you that this technique can be dangerous and has been known to lead to interviewees smirking or giggling for no apparent reason in front of perplexed interviewers. A variation on the theme is to imagine the interviewer as a toothbrush, or something equally ludicrous. Try it out on someone else in another situation and see if it works for you.

Tactics in Dealing with Different Types of Question

There are a number of different types of question you will meet in an interview. The main ones are listed below along with some hints on dealing with them. Putting this into practice may be difficult first time round, but you will grow more adept with each interview.

Closed questions

These are the ones we talked about earlier (p. 29), which require only 'yes' or 'no', or similarly brief answers. Nothing difficult about that for you. But you may find that some inexperienced, or just ineffective, interviewers ask so many questions of this type that you do not get a chance to say very much. The only way closed questions can cause problems is by stopping you from putting across information you feel might help your chances of getting the job. In those circumstances, you have to take the initiative by giving more information than is strictly called for by the question. This is discussed further below, in the section on helping less competent interviewers.

Open questions

This is where the interviewer gives you the chance to talk, by asking questions like

'What do you like doing in your spare time?'
'Tell me something about your time at college.'

All well and good: you can use the opportunity to put over the things you want to communicate about yourself. If you have prepared properly, you will know what you want to get across and will concentrate on that. If you have not bothered to prepare and have not thought about the likely questions, then open-ended ones can be a problem: they give you so much scope for answering that you sometimes do not know where to begin, what to put in and what to leave out.

Hypothetical questions

No, this does not mean questions you might be asked. It is the name given to questions of the 'What would you do *if* . . . ?' variety; questions that put you in an imaginary situation and ask you how you would deal with it. For example:

> 'Say you were in charge of some staff who were older than yourself and who resented having a younger supervisor, how would you deal with them?'

These questions are of very dubious value, mainly because what a person says they would do in no way guarantees that they would act that way if really faced with the situation. Also, the situation is only sketchily outlined, and that is what you must emphasise in your answer; in real life you would know *much* more about the people and/or the situation concerned, and this knowledge would almost certainly influence the way in which you tackled the matter. Having made that point tactfully, you can go on to answer the question as best you can. If the interviewer does not like the particular line of thought you give in answer to this hypothetical question, at least he has been made aware of the fact that a truly accurate answer is impossible. Another answer that is sometimes appropriate, particularly if the interviewer asks you to say how you would sort out a particular kind of problem, is to preface your reply with a statement to the effect that you would hope you could avoid that kind of problem arising anyway (if, of course, it seems avoidable to you). You might then say 'But if it did, then I would . . .'.

Multiple questions

Even the most experienced and well-trained interviewers succumb to the error of asking multiple questions now and then. As the term implies, these are questions delivered in a string – you get not one question, but several at once. For example:

'What sort of things do you like doing in your time off? Do you read much? or go to the cinema – have you seen this latest film that everyone is talking about?'

Sometimes half a dozen questions cascade out like this in a single sentence. The interviewer starts with one idea, but as he asks the question, he changes his mind either about what precisely he wants to know or how to put it. The result is something of a mess, the interviewee not knowing quite which question to answer, or whether to answer all of them. Very often, the first question asked is the best one – the interviewer should bite his lip if he feels the need to elaborate on it. You could answer the first one and help him, or answer the very last one, which usually gives the least information; if you do not really want to talk about the topic much, answer the question that gives the least scope. Multiple questions, if you think fast enough, give you the chance to try to limit or expand how much you say on a topic by choosing which element(s) of them to answer. The greatest danger is that of becoming confused and trying to answer all of the questions at once; in this case, your answer becomes as ill-thought-out as the question.

Leading questions
These have been discussed on p. 30. The interviewer indicates the kind of answer he expects when he asks a leading question. For example:

'You will have to move around a lot in this job; does that appeal to you?'

Most people when presented with a question like that not unnaturally tell the interviewer what he expects or wants to hear. If you feel especially truthful and do not want to give the answer he expects, then you could go ahead and surprise him; at least he might give you credit for your independence. Generally speaking, though, it is best not to rock the boat: go where leading questions lead you, unless you feel it very important not to.

Unexpected or difficult questions

These obviously take many shapes and forms, but one of the common needs interviewees have in the face of them is time to think out an answer. First, you should, of course, give yourself a moment to think rather than trying to start your reply immediately, whether or not you have any idea of what you are really saying. On the other hand, you can only take a second or two before starting to reply – much longer than that and you may appear a bit dim. This does not allow much time for thought, so is there any way you can buy more time? One useful little device is to say something along the lines of 'How exactly do you mean?' – a tactic that makes the interviewer rephrase the question so as to make it clearer, thus allowing you more time to sort out your answer. However, you must use this technique very sparingly, not more than twice in any one interview, and only for the most difficult sorts of question (otherwise you will simply be thought a bit dim for not understanding the first time round).

Some questions asked in interviews are not just difficult, they are almost impossible to answer. One interviewer I heard asked a candidate how he thought we could cure inflation, to which the candidate reasonably replied that, since the government had failed to do so, he did not think he had much chance of coming up with a solution to it either. Questions that go beyond what you can reasonably hope to answer in the limited time of an interview, or that defy any clear answer anyway, should be gently and diplomatically pointed out as such to the interviewer in the course of attempting to answer them.

One tactic you should *not* try is being evasive. Dealing with a difficult question by answering one slightly different from that asked might work just once, but doing it persistently simply irritates interviewers and will work against you.

The Sound of Silence

A few seconds of silence in an interview seem like an eternity, both to interviewers and to candidates. The important thing is not to be panicked by it. As has been pointed out already, it is better to take a second or two, to think out an answer if need be rather than to launch into an answer prematurely. Silences are a problem for the interviewer as well. Sometimes they come about because the interviewer has forgotten what he was going to say or simply cannot think of anything else to ask, which usually causes him some discomfort. And silence on the part of an interviewee following a question leaves the interviewer with a difficult decision to make: does he assume that the interviewee is just thinking out his answer or that he is completely nonplussed by the question and in need of rescue? The interviewer has to know when a pregnant pause becomes an embarrassed silence.

Some interviewers do actually use silence to put pressure on you. They ask a question, and then remain silent when you have finished answering. This unsettles a lot of candidates, and, assuming that more is required, they start desperately trying to elaborate on what has generally been a perfectly adequate answer. Do not fall into this nasty little trap: if the interviewer remains silent when you have finished answering, you remain silent too, even if it is difficult to do so. If the interviewer wants you to elaborate further, or seeks clarification of what you have already said, let him ask for it.

Assertive Behaviour

The central theme of this book is that you do not have to be totally passive in an interview. Indeed, you can do a lot to help your chances by actively trying to get across the information you want to communicate. In other words, you must assert yourself to a degree. The importance of this is demonstrated by an American research study that showed that interviewers who saw passive, unassertive candidates tended to assume that they were unambitious, non-competitive, emotionally unstable and illogical – irrespective of anything they actually said! So in interviews it is not just what you say, it is how you say it. Some of the main aspects of assertive behaviour are dealt with in this section.

Your attitude

Just how assertive should one be? Are you expected to 'sell' yourself directly and unambiguously in an interview? Usually not, though there are some interviewers who invite you to do so by asking questions like 'What have you got to offer us, Miss X?', or 'Now, tell me why do you think you will do a good job for us?'. Where this happens, you know where you stand and can quite shamelessly start 'selling'. However, most interviewers, and candidates, do draw back from anything quite as blunt as this approach. What candidates must usually do, it seems, is to project a modest, slightly submissive image, while somehow making sure that their good points are noted. The latter often has to be achieved by the interviewee making sure that their good points do come out in the interview irrespective of whether the interviewer asks the right questions or not. But this must be done gently, unobtrusively and without any hint of bragging or overtly trying to control the interview.

Apart from this, there are two other aspects of one's attitude in an interview that we should talk about.

* *Enthusiasm.* This is vital. You must look and sound as though you are interested and keen both about the job and even about the interview itself. You know the difference there is in your face and voice when talking about something that really interests you and that you like, as compared to when you are talking of something you dislike and find boring. You must aim for the former in an interview. Lack of interest or enthusiasm will convey itself to the interviewer very quickly, and will probably be taken as a lack of commitment on your part, with gloomy results.

* *Humour.* Is one supposed to be very serious at interviews? Being fairly serious and earnest will probably not go against you, providing you do not keep a stony face when the interviewer cracks a joke. But some sign of a sense of humour can work very much in your favour. No one can tell you how to go about this, of course, as it obviously depends on the opportunity given. Forced humour out of context will not be received very favourably, and nor will excessive flippancy. So it is a question of your own judgement as to whether or not you inject an occasional flash of wit into the proceedings; if done in the appropriate way, it works very well.

Talking

If an interview is being conducted well, you should not really need to assert yourself in terms of the amount of talking you do, as you will be doing most of it anyway. If it is conducted badly, with a lot of closed questions, this gives you less scope to talk, as we noted earlier – and the advice given earlier (p. 84) holds. What we should look at here are other aspects of asserting yourself when talking.

* A very basic one is speaking up. An amazing number of candidates (probably through anxiety) speak so quietly and softly that the interviewer has difficulty catching all they say. You really must speak in a clear, audible and as confident a voice as possible.

* Remember also what we said a moment ago about enthusiasm: let it show in your voice; you cannot assert yourself very effectively if you are speaking in a weary monotone, or in a nervous, hasty babble.

* You can do too much talking sometimes, and this is something to guard against. Do not let your answers ramble on too long. Again, this is something you have to judge for yourself, but a look at the interviewer's face will sometimes give you a clue!

* The other point to bring in here, though it has little to do with assertive behaviour as such, is your *accent*. If you have a strong regional, or even national, accent it may cross your mind that it could be better to disguise it as best you can. It is true that some interviewers react badly to accents different from their own, but generally one has too much else on one's mind in an interview to try and talk in a different way as well. So be yourself, with the exception only of someone who just does not seem to understand what you are saying, in which case you may need to speak a little more slowly.

Checking and clarifying

Some interviewees are very reluctant to interrupt an interviewer, and generally this is quite right. However, if the interviewer has clearly misunderstood what you said in an answer, you should make that clear. You can say something like 'I am sorry, that's not really what I meant.'

If you do not understand what the interviewer has asked, you should seek clarification rather than attempt an answer to what you think they might be asking. All you have to do is say something like 'I don't quite get your meaning', or 'I am not quite sure I understand the question.'

Arguing with the interviewer

Interviewees often wonder whether it is wise to dis-agree with an interviewer, still less to argue. Well, it can go either way. Most interviewers seem to want appli-cants to be politely attentive and agreeable, but a few like to provoke applicants to see if they are able to look after themselves under stress. In general, it is best to avoid firm expressions of disagreement with inter-viewers, except where they get you to express your views on a topic and then present an opposing argu-ment. This is quite common, the interviewer aiming to see how well you can argue a case and support your viewpoint. He may not himself actually believe the opposing views he puts to you, but he will play the role of devil's advocate if necessary. However, most exchanges are more like debates than arguments and the interviewer will remain friendly and businesslike; there is little danger of mistaking this kind of exchange for one where the interviewer tries to provoke you or attack your views in a more personal way (in which case one often hears phrases like 'You don't mean to tell me that . . .', 'You are not seriously suggesting . . .', 'You seem to have made a bit of a mess of that', etc.). In similar vein, a few interviewers use sarcasm as a way of provoking the candidate, a lamentable strategy.

So, in general, do not look for arguments, but if one is 'offered' you should remain cool, defend your point of view in an agreeable way and be willing to acknowledge *some* sense in opposing views without actually accepting them.

Volunteering and seeking information
If you have prepared properly, you will know what information you want the interviewer to have about you at the end of the interview – the good points you have identified. Some of these will come out naturally in the course of a good interview, but the rest you need to feed in yourself. Answer questions in such a way that you can work into them the points *you* have decided you want to get across. You can also do a little gentle 'steering' of the discussion.

- For example, if you are asked whether you ever go to the theatre, when in fact you are really much more keen and knowledgeable about the cinema, you need not just answer 'No' and hope that the interviewer will ask you about films. You can answer 'No, my interests are much more in the cinema; I go quite a lot'; the interviewer will follow up from there.

- Do not miss opportunities of this kind for volunteering information on your strengths, and if no opportunity arises in respect of some of them, then you might be able to create it.

- For example, if you have some experience of working with computers that you feel is relevant to your application but that has not come out in the interview, you could introduce it by asking a question like 'Are there any opportunities for work in the computer field – I've already had some experience of that and enjoyed it.'

The questions candidates are normally allowed to ask at the end of the interview offer a considerable opportunity to present any further information in this way.

Finally!
Do not voluntarily offer information on what you see as your weaker aspects. Apart from a tendency by some interviewers to give such negative points undue weight in their assessment, your idea of what is unsatisfactory may be at odds with the general standard of work (or whatever) in that area; in other words, you may be better than you think.

Helping the less competent interviewer
Many of the assertive forms of behaviour already mentioned will help interviewers who are not very good at their task. By helping them you will help yourself. So by all means expand on the closed questions they ask, instead of just answering very briefly. Give them plenty of leads to follow in your answers, and if they finally dry up, rescue them by saying something like:

'Perhaps, to get a fuller picture of me, you ought to know about . . .'
'Would it be helpful to you if I said something about . . .'.

Also, if they fail to ask you if you want to ask questions of your own at the end of the interview, you can bring it to their notice that you would like to ask one or two things yourself. Less competent interviewers are usually grateful for candidates who gently take the initiative.

Non-Verbal Behaviour

A great deal has been said and written about non-verbal behaviour, 'body language', expressive movement and so on. Certainly, the way we look and move can tell somebody else a lot about us, and often it gives a better guide to a person's feelings than what they actually say. The importance of non-verbal behaviour in the interview is, however, not altogether clear. Some research findings have indicated it as being an important part of the communication process, while others have shown it has having relatively little influence on the interaction between interviewer and candidate. To be on the safe side, I will assume here that it *can* affect interview judgements and will use the research findings to guide you as to what is and what is not advisable.

Some advice has already been given on this, in particular the desirability of smiling at the interviewer when you first meet him. However, the rest of what needs to be said can be dealt with under the headings of posture and eye contact.

Posture

This to some extent is dependent on the kind of chair you are given to sit in, but in general you should try to sit comfortably and reasonably *upright* – no sprawling or slouching. As we said earlier, comfort is important to your relaxation in the interview, but it must not be at the expense of creating a lazy image. It is better to lean slightly *forward* than to lean back; it communicates interest and attentiveness (this works both ways – I have seen whole boards of interviewers visibly sway forward when an attractive female applicant walks into the room!)

Otherwise serene candidates often give themselves away by what they do with their hands and arms in an interview. Some grip the arms of the chair so tightly that their knuckles show white. Others gesticulate far too much, or continually shift the position of their arms. You can put your arms in just about any comfortable position, but do not keep shifting them; a lot of fidgeting seems to irritate some interviewers and is to be avoided. Also to be avoided is the habit of speaking with a hand in front of your mouth (playing with a beard, for instance) and any other mannerism that is likely to trigger off one of the interviewer's prejudices, e.g. head scratching, thumb picking, finger drumming.

So, as far as posture is concerned, the prescription is to keep fairly upright but leaning forward *slightly*, with low peripheral movement and as much relaxation as you can manage.

You may like to find the most comfortable way of achieving this before you go for an interview. Just place a chair in front of a mirror and see what position you feel most comfortable in while still meeting the requirements given above.

Eye contact

This term refers to occasions when two individuals are looking each other straight in the eye. Research has shown us quite a lot about patterns of eye contact and how they can influence our responses to one another. In normal conversation, the pattern is something like this. Individual A talks and sometimes looks (which means eye contact in this description) at individual B, who listens and sometimes looks at A (see (1) in diagram). When A stops talking, he looks at B, whereupon B generally averts his eyes from A while he plans his answer (2). When B commences his answer, he looks at A from time to time to see that A is attending and to note reactions, while A is listening and sometimes looking at B (3).

This is more or less the pattern you will encounter in interviews. The next time you have a conversation with someone, try to notice how this pattern of eye contact works – it is a very consistent one. The important thing is that you do have eye contact with the interviewer. The amount of eye contact that takes place between people seems to be related to some extent to how much they like each other. This does not mean, however, that

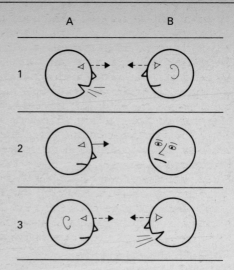

you must transfix the interviewer with an unwavering stare, as though you had never seen anything quite like it before.

> Look him in the eye when you first meet, look at him most of the time when he is talking and look at him some of the time when you are talking to him. The one thing not to do is to avoid the eyes of the interviewer most of the time.

For Ladies Only
We might call this section 'sex and the interview'. There is a lot of research evidence showing that women are generally more ready to disclose information about themselves than are men. My own investigations – and my experience as an interviewer – suggest that this is true in the interview situation as well. They seem to be more open, more honest and less manipulative than men doing interviews. Not that men are particularly secretive about their positive qualities – the real difference is in the attitude to revealing anything that might be received unfavourably, where the men seem much

more inclined to say only what they have to (much as was advised earlier on p. 93) but the women tend to be relatively open. As an example, I well remember one 30-year-old lady telling me, quite unsolicited, all about the affair she was having with her boss, who was over 60, and extolling the virtues of older men. This was in an interview for a job that involved highly sensitive overseas postings where discretion was essential! Since I was only a few years older than she was, it is unlikely that she said this just to make me feel better. Presumably, she was simply being very self-disclosing. Faced with this or something like it (one has to admit that it is a fairly extreme example), does the interviewer assess the candidate favourably on the grounds of honesty, or unfavourably on the grounds of poor judgement, being indiscreet, etc.? Given that we have already observed how interviewers usually attach a heavy weighting to anything that might be construed as unfavourable, it is difficult to conclude other than that such openness is more likely to reduce the candidate's chances than to enhance them.

So, the message for women when facing the interview is clear: take a leaf out of the men's book and be a little more reserved and cautious in what you say about yourself.

The Interviewers' Behaviour

The interview is very much a two-way communication process. Interviewers will be noting your behaviour (after all, that is what he is there for) and you will be noting theirs, sometimes mistakenly. Candidates are often quite strongly affected by what they see, or think they see, interviewers doing during the course of the interview. Note-taking is a prime example. Many interviewers take notes during the interview, and very sensibly too as they will be hard-pressed to remember everything they hear about a series of candidates. Unfortunately some candidates get upset and think that something is wrong if interviewers start taking 'evidence' like this. In fact, you should be glad if notes are taken: the interviewers are doing their job properly! Another thing candidates pick up are the signals some-times given to each other by different members of an interviewing board. All these should be ignored; they have no significance for the interviewee in terms of his assessment. The signals are usually to tell one board member that his allotted time questioning the candidate is up or almost up.

More disturbing for interviewees is the feedback they get from how interviewers look rather than any-thing they do. I stressed the importance of enthusiasm and interest on the part of the candidate a few pages ago. Well, interviewers should really be able to project a little of this too, but they do not always do so. Often this is quite understandable as one interview follows an-other in what may be a period of days spent inter-viewing. Sometimes the interest, let alone energy and concentration, sags and interviewers let it show on their faces. On no account must you let this deter you or dampen your own motivation. A persistent lack of enthusiasm from an interviewer is not necessarily an implied criticism of you – it usually stems from other things. Indeed, if interviewers are fatigued or slightly bored with perhaps their fifth interview that day, it is all the more important that you do appear keen, in-terested and enthusiastic. Boredom and lack of interest breed boredom and lack of interest, but you cannot afford to let this happen.

One final point about interviewers, and this is where sex rears its ugly head again. There is a tendency amongst some candidates, particularly the males, to relax a little more when faced with a female interviewer. It is as if the fact that the interview is being conducted by a woman makes the whole thing less threatening. Partly this reflects the attitude of the candidate, and partly the skill of many female interviewers in settling down the interviewees and establishing rapport with them. Your approach should be much the same regard-less of the sex of the person doing the interview; do not be deluded into thinking that a female interviewer means you are in for an easier time – it may feel more comfortable, but the assessment will be just as thorough, if not more so.

Closing the Interview

The final period of an interview is often the one used by interviewers to let you ask any questions you may have about the job or the organisation, and you should have prepared these. Sometimes the interviewer will ask whether there is anything he has missed out or not asked that he should. Obviously if there is anything else you feel may work to your credit that has not been covered, you will bring it up now. Even if you are not given this kind of opportunity by the interviewer, you can create it for yourself by saying something to the effect 'One thing that has not come out today and which you might find helpful to know is that I . . .'.

Once again, as you say goodbye you should look the interviewer in the eye (or, if it is a board, a swift glance at each one of them) and smile. Sometimes the interviewer will offer a hand to shake, which you will of course take even though in some cases you will feel more like shaking him warmly by the throat!

Summary of Advice

The main points made in this chapter may be summarised in the form of two lists, one of 'Do's' and one of 'Don't's'. You might like to look back at the brief quiz you did on p. 81 and think to what extent you would want to modify your answers; look at them in relation to these 'golden rules':

DO

☞ Smile at the interviewers and look them in the eye when you meet and when you leave.

☞ Maintain lots of eye contact in the interview.

☞ Sit upright and lean slightly forward.

☞ Take your time in answering questions.

☞   Look and sound both enthusiastic and interested.

☞   Speak up.

☞   Get across information that will help your case.

☞   Carefully qualify your answers to 'hypothetical' questions.

☞   Try to help interviewers who are in difficulty.

☞   Be willing to defend your viewpoint in a friendly way.

☞   Ask one or two questions of your own if the chance arises.

DO NOT

☞   Slouch in the chair.

☞   Fidget.

☞   Panic if there is a period of silence (do not talk for the sake of talking).

☞   Smoke (unless invited or unless really desperate) or chew anything.

☞   Be evasive in your answers, or try to bluff.

☞   Boast or 'sell' yourself directly unless invited to.

☞   Argue with the interviewer in any heated way.

☞   Allow yourself to be put off if the interviewer seems unenthusiastic or bored.

☞   Speak too quickly.

☞   Volunteer information about your real or imagined deficiencies.

☞   Take it easy when faced with a female interviewer.

7

The Use of Psychological Tests and Other Techniques

Multiple Procedures in Assessment

We have seen that interviews are beset by problems and that they tend to be a rather poor way of selecting people for jobs. This has led to the search for other ways of comparing individuals and choosing between them. The interview will probably continue to be used for the reasons mentioned in Chapter 1, but increasingly it is being supplemented by other techniques. These include:

* psychological tests of various kinds,

* group discussion tasks,

* certain objective performance measures on simulated work tasks.

Sometimes all of these may be used together in what is called an *assessment centre procedure*, something which is becoming more popular with organisations these days. The Civil Service Selection Board has actually been using a multiple procedure of this kind for many years and has a proven record of its effectiveness.

In this short chapter, I will try to describe some of the kinds of supplementary assessment procedures you may encounter along with the interview. Apart from saying what they are, I will try to explain the main points about their use and, when appropriate, give some advice. The philosophy here, as in the case of interviews, is that they cause less anxiety for people who know what to expect and why they are being given.

The Use of Psychological Tests

The use of these tests evokes strong emotional reactions from many people; some quite enjoy them while others seem to either fear them or ridicule them (or both). Much of the abuse hurled at them is extremely ill-informed, which is not really surprising since psychological testing is a far more complex and sophisticated field than it appears on the surface. The value of these tests in predicting success in work settings is well established, and their use is increasing; they are here to stay because they work reasonably well.

As long as the psychological test is properly used, you have no reason to fear it. Selection decisions are seldom based on test data alone, and the test data can sometimes help offset a bad interview performance (though it rarely seems to work in the other direction you will be glad to know). The best general advice one can give is to urge you to get some *practice* at taking tests. This will make relatively little difference to your performance under non-stressful circumstances (practice on ability tests only raises scores a limited amount), but it may make quite a lot of difference to the way you *feel* if you have to take such tests as part of a selection procedure. That is rather more stressful, and if the phenomenon of test anxiety rears its head your performance can suffer, so that you do not give a fair impression of your ability. However, if you have previously worked through examples of the kind of test items you are likely to encounter, you will probably feel much happier and more confident about them. Two books which may well help in this respect are *Know your own IQ* by H. J. Eysenck and *Know your own personality* by Glen Wilson and H. J. Eysenck (both published by Penguin). These contain plenty of examples of items typical of ability and personality tests.

INTELLIGENCE TESTS

Tests of intelligence take many different forms according to the aspect of intelligence being assessed, the characteristics of the group being assessed and the purposes of the assessment. The variation in the content of these tests is so great that any proper discussion of them is beyond the scope of this book. But one important point you should keep in mind about them is that they can be of some help to you if you are lacking in formal academic or other qualifications. Often an intelligence test will indicate that someone who has few exam passes is really very bright, thus directing the interviewers toward finding out why the educational attainment was low relative to the individual's potential as shown by the tests. In this way, test data can offset some of the disadvantages of a poor or deprived background by giving a clearer picture of a person's ability than do his school attainments. Many tests can do this because they are thought to measure basic reasoning power; they may include non-verbal items that do not rely on how well an individual has been taught English or Mathematics (at home or at school). On the debit side, however, it must also be admitted that some psychological tests have a cultural bias that can in some cases put members of minority racial groups at a disadvantage (though this can to an extent be offset by the length of time the individual has lived in a Western culture).

PERSONALITY MEASURES

One must first make it clear that a psychologist's use of the term personality is not the same as the layman's; the psychological concept of personality does not involve ideas about one person having more personality than another, or one person having a better or worse personality than someone else. In personality tests there are no 'right' answers as such. The replies are used to give a picture of the individual's enduring traits, dispositions and motives. Again, there are many types of personality test. (Incidentally, they should not, strictly speaking, be called 'tests' – because there are no 'right' or 'wrong' answers as such.) The most frequently encountered is the questionnaire that takes the person's replies on anything from 50 to 500 questions and processes them in such a way as to yield scores on various traits or other aspects of personality. Less often encountered is the projective type of personality test. This is where you are presented with an ambiguous or abstract stimulus, e.g. an ink-blot or a picture of some domestic scene, and asked to say something about it (in the case of an ink-blot, what it reminds you of; in the case of a picture, make up a story about what is happening). The idea is that in responding, you 'project' important aspects of your personality in your interpretation of the stimulus. However, there are serious problems associated with the use of projective tests and their value as selection devices is highly questionable except in a small minority of rather special cases.

Taking the Tests
There is little more that can be said in regard to **intelligence tests**.

* *Always* read the instructions carefully – do not hurry over them.

* If you are taking a test that is timed, you have to work out your own strategy: working quickly and increasing the chance of errors or working more slowly with less chance of errors but less chance of completing the test too. As a general rule it is not good to go so slowly that many items are not attempted. What you can do is to leave any items that cause you particular difficulty until

you have completed the rest and then return to them if
you have any time left.

---

* When you are actually doing the tests concentrate on
the task in hand, and try to ignore any other job
applicants who may be taking the same tests as you
(they are often administered to groups of people together), or you may start worrying if they seem to be
working much more quickly than you or acting differently in any other way. Do *not* concern yourself with
them, or whether they are doing better than you –
simply get on with the task in hand and keep your head
down!

Personality measures are a different matter all together.
They are usually open to a number of distorting influences, an important one being social desirability.
This is the tendency some people show to answer
questions in the way that they think will put them in
the best light: answering questions in the 'right' way.
This may or may not be a conscious phenomenon, but
it is certainly a real one. Related to this is the more
serious problem of deliberate faking. People have different ideas of what personality questionnaires are
measuring and of what 'sort' of personality the
organisation is trying to recruit; they sometimes try to
present themselves on such questionnaires in the way
that will increase their chances of acceptance rather
than in the way that will give the truest picture of their
personality. Many studies have shown that job applicants are sometimes less than truthful when doing
personality tests. Even psychiatric patients diagnosed
as schizophrenic can manipulate the impression they
give of themselves on these devices, so it is not surprising that psychologically normal individuals are prone
to do so as well. Some writers have even given advice
on the kind of personality it is safest to project on tests.
For example, William Whyte Jr in his famous book *The
organization man* suggested all applicants taking personality tests should repeat the following to themselves:

> I loved my father and my mother, but my father a little bit more. I like things pretty much the way they are. I never worry much about anything. I do not care for books or music much. I love my wife and children. I do not let them get in the way of company work.

Clearly the idea is to present as conventional an image as possible. While this advice from Whyte is quite amusing and contains some sense, it is also a little dangerous. Not all organisations need or seek the same kind of personality profile. Guessing the kind of personality characteristics a company is seeking from its applicants is a hazardous business because of the wide difference between them on some things. Moreover, most personality tests contain special items for detecting people who are either showing social desirability effects or blatantly faking. Some of these 'lie scores' and other devices are fairly easy to spot, but many are not. They are thus another danger for anyone trying deliberately to present themselves in a particular way they think will go down well. All in all, honesty probably remains the best policy on personality measures.

Other Selection Techniques

When appointing people to senior positions, or to posts that probably will in time lead on to quite senior jobs, it is increasingly common to find that the candidates are observed and assessed actually performing a range of tasks. The qualities to be noted from these exercises are specified beforehand as being relevant to the job and often cover things that are felt to be inadequately assessed by the interview alone, e.g. business sense, administrative skills, leadership, expression on paper, and so on.

Group discussion

This is the most frequent technique and involves putting anything from four to eight candidates together in a group and giving them one or more topics to discuss. Often they have to come to a group decision or solution to a problem posed. While the candidates are discussing the topic provided, observers note each individual's contribution to the discussion. The aspects of behaviour being assessed vary according to the organisation and the setting, but obviously relate to an individual's functioning as part of a team.

> The most important thing to remember if you find yourself in a group exercise of this kind is to *contribute* something to the discussion. You cannot be given much credit for saying nothing!

Try to forget about those observers watching you and concentrate on taking part wholeheartedly. The other candidates are all in the same boat and probably feel just as daunted and nervous as you do. You should try to:

- put your own ideas forward

- speak up clearly

- say something early on in the exercise

- be supportive to your fellow candidates

- avoid looking at the observers

- be pleasant in manner.

The 'in-tray' exercise

This is an approach that is growing in popularity. It consists of a series of documents designed to resemble the kind of paperwork problems that managers in those organisations would encounter very frequently. The candidates are usually given some time to study background details of the organisation before tackling the problems and taking appropriate action within the time allowed. Their handling of these tasks is rated on various aspects of effectiveness. Faced with tasks of this kind, *the golden rule is to judge your time carefully*. Make a quick review of what you have to read through and what you are being required to do, and then allocate your time accordingly; do not just start at the beginning and put your head down without trying to assess what is of greater or lesser importance.

Physical tasks
Some selection procedures involve candidates in group tasks of a more physical nature. This is particularly true of officer selection in the armed forces. A typical task would be for a group of candidates, with one designated as leader, to have to manoeuvre a heavy object over a series of obstacles with the aid of only rudimentary equipment (generally the candidates have to produce some novel ideas on how to utilise this equipment to achieve the set target).

All of these procedures focus on certain aspects of behaviour more closely than does the interview, and the value of the assessments made from them can be considerable. They may tell you less overall about a person, but what they do tell you is more specific, easier to relate to particular facets of the job being applied for and generally more reliable as a form of evidence. As indicated at the beginning of this chapter, the best results are obtained when one or more of these procedures are used in conjunction with the interview and the information from all the different sources is pooled for the final decision.

Feedback on Tests and Other Selection Techniques
It is increasingly common to find that organisations that operate these more sophisticated assessment techniques will offer you feedback on your performance. Even if they do not mention provision for it, you might find it worthwhile asking if they would give you some indication of how you fared. They certainly *should* give you feedback – you will probably have been required to put a good deal of time and effort into their selection

procedure, so the least they can do is to give you something in return. Feedback can be extremely useful to you; it should help considerably when tackling similar situations in the future.

Do not be too downhearted if you feel you have not done very well on tests, group exercises or the like. They may seem very thorough and comprehensive as ways of assessing you (and, compared to just an interview, they are), but even they are by no means perfect. They will certainly miss many aspects of your personality and talent, though hopefully not those most relevant to the jobs in question. And whatever picture they present of you is only valid for a while. People change and develop, often improving significantly in some areas of their abilities. Indeed, some candidates encountering these selection exercises for the first time find them a bit of a shock, and given a second chance on a later occasion acquit themselves much more impressively. *So if at first you don't succeed, try again!*

Summary of Advice

☞ Try to get some practice in taking psychological tests.

☞ When taking intelligence and ability tests, read through the instructions carefully and at your own pace.

☞ If there is anything in the instructions that you are unsure about, ask the person administering the tests.

☞ Do not work too slowly; if you find a test item difficult, leave it and come back to it later if you have time.

☞ Take no notice of how any other people also doing the test seem to be getting on with them.

☞ Answer personality measures honestly.

☞ In group exercises, contribute your ideas as clearly and confidently as possible, and with a pleasant manner.

☞ Faced with 'in-tray' or similar written exercises, get a quick overview of the task and judge the allocation of your time to different parts of it carefully.

☞ Try to get some feedback on your performance on tests or exercises after the selection day.

8

Reviewing Your Performance

Analysing and Interpreting the Interview

We learn best from experience, and to get the most out of your experience of interviews you need to analyse and interpret them as soon afterwards as possible (otherwise your memory will obscure much of the detail). Do not wait until you hear the outcome of your application, because quite apart from the likelihood of forgetting what went on your later perceptions of the interview may be highly coloured by your acceptance or rejection. So think about it within twenty-four hours.

To help you do this in a fairly structured way, you might like to use the review guide given here. If you think about these questions in relation to your interview you should reap considerable benefit from it as a learning experience. And as far as this is concerned, it really does not matter whether the interview turns out to be a successful one for you or not; even if you find you have been appointed, there will be other interviews in the future, either for promotion or when you change jobs.

Post-interview
Review Guide

First impressions:
- What do you feel your chances of success are?
- What were your overall reactions? What sort of experience was it – enjoyable, tense, unpleasant, challenging, or what?
- Did the interviewers seem friendly and interested?
- Was the interview fairly and competently conducted?
- If not, what do you think they should have done differently, and why?
- What topics were covered? (Write down all that you can remember as soon as you come out of the interview.)

Your performance:
- Did you manage to stay (or at least *appear*) relaxed and confident in manner?
- Were you able to demonstrate an adequate knowledge of the organisation and the job (if it was required)?
- Which topics had you anticipated, and which came as unexpected?
- What did you feel you put across well? What do you feel you could have improved upon and how?
- Were there any questions you found particularly difficult? Why?
- How did you cope with them?
- What sort of impression do you feel you made on the interviewer(s)?
- Having answered all the above questions and thought about them, is your answer to the first question in this review guide still the same?

Looking ahead:
- What did you learn from this interview about presenting yourself?
- If you need to go for further interviews, what aspects of your interview performance will you try to improve, and how?

The Outcome of the Interview
If you get the job, little more needs to be said, apart from congratulating you, and reminding you –

* Do not forget to let your referrees know the outcome, and thank them.

However, few people get what they are after with just one interview. You have to accept that no matter how well you do in both preparing and presenting yourself, someone else may have done just as well and have formal qualifications superior to your own. Not being offered a job should not be taken as a reproach; it is inevitable that a lot of people interviewed as part of a given selection process will not get jobs, because more are interviewed than there are vacancies. There is no disgrace (as some people give the impression of feeling) in admitting that some people are better suited or better qualified for a job than you are. Besides which, some candidates are rejected because they are too *good* for the job!

So there is certainly no point in blaming yourself unless you just did not bother to prepare for the interview and took a passive role in it. Taking steps to improve your chances next time is much more constructive. Reviewing your performance is one important activity that has already been mentioned. Another possible measure is to contact the interviewers, usually by writing a *polite* letter, though sometimes by phone if you think they would not mind, and asking them what it was about your application or interview performance that let you down, if anything (someone might just have been better). Where the interview concerned was one of a considerable number carried out as part of a large-scale recruitment exercise, you probably would not be able to do this. But in many other cases it is worth a try and can sometimes provide useful feedback, though one should treat what is said with some caution as the interviewers may not be entirely frank in their comments or may simply have made their decision to reject you on poor grounds.

Another word of warning: be careful when phoning or writing to interviewers that you do not in any way give the impression of asking them to 'justify' a selection decision that you feel aggrieved at.

Failing to get a job from two or three interviews should not cause alarm or despondency, but if the lack of success continues much beyond that, it may call for a more fundamental reappraisal. Clearly, if you have been getting the interviews then you are definitely in the running as far as the organisation is concerned. So what is going wrong? It may be that you are applying for jobs where the competition is particularly intense and where it would be quite common to find people having numerous interviews before being 'lucky' (and there is often an element of luck in interviews). On the other hand, you may be putting yourself over in the interview just as well as anyone but not striking the interviewers as being the right type of person for this type of job, and they may be right. So, after a prolonged period without success you should, perhaps, think of getting some expert advice from a careers officer or from a private vocational counselling practitioner. Ideally, you would have been given this sort of help in the first place, but this is all too rarely the case. Better late than never, though, and seeking guidance after a series of rejections might well throw some new light on the problem and lead to a better fit between your qualities and skills and the requirements of the jobs for which you apply.

The majority of readers of this book are unlikely to experience repeated rejections; the very fact that you have read it suggests that you are approaching the business of seeking the job you want with commitment and vigour. The effort you are putting in now will be repaid many times over when you find the right job. You have taken a lot of advice in the course of reading through this book, and if you combine it with something much more important – namely, your own wit and intelligence – you will be in a position to tackle that all-important interview in the positive manner it needs for success.

Summary of Advice

☞ Review your interview performance as soon as possible after the interview.

☞ Identify areas you need to improve on next time and plan how to go about it.

☞ Inform your referees of the outcome and thank them.

☞ If you are not offered the job, try to get some feedback on why – but be polite in doing so!

☞ Should you experience a prolonged lack of success, seek a second opinion: are you aiming for the right kind of job?

The HOW TO Series

All these books are available at your local bookshop or newsagent, or can be ordered direct by post. Just tick the titles you want and fill in the form below.

Name ....

Address ....

....

....

Write to Unwin Cash Sales, PO Box 11, Falmouth, Cornwall TR10 9EN.

Please enclose remittance to the value of the cover price plus:

UK: 60p for the first book plus 25p for the second book, thereafter, 15p for each additional book ordered to a maximum charge of £1.90.

BFPO and EIRE: 60p for the first book plus 25p for the second book and 15p per copy for the next 7 books and thereafter 9p per book.

OVERSEAS INCLUDING EIRE: £1.25 for the first book plus 75p for the second book and 28p for each additional book.

Unwin Paperbacks reserve the right to show new retail prices on covers which may differ from those previously advertised in the text or elsewhere. Postage rates are also subject to revision.